New Directions for
Higher Education

Martin Kramer and
Judith Block McLaughlin
CO-EDITORS-IN-CHIEF

The First Year and Beyond: Rethinking the Challenge of Collegiate Transition

Betsy O. Barefoot

EDITOR

Number 144 • Winter 2008
Jossey-Bass
San Francisco

THE FIRST YEAR AND BEYOND: RETHINKING THE CHALLENGE OF
COLLEGIATE TRANSITION
Betsy O. Barefoot (ed.)
New Directions for Higher Education, no. 144
Martin Kramer, Judith Block McLaughlin, Co-Editors-in-Chief

Microfilm copies of issues and articles are available in 16mm and 35mm, as well as microfiche in 105mm, through University Microfilms Inc., 300 North Zeeb Road, Ann Arbor, Michigan 48106-1346.

NEW DIRECTIONS FOR HIGHER EDUCATION (ISSN 0271-0560, electronic ISSN 1536-0741) is part of The Jossey-Bass Higher and Adult Education Series and is published quarterly by Wiley Subscription Services, Inc., A Wiley Company, at Jossey-Bass, 989 Market Street, San Francisco, California 94103-1741. Periodicals Postage Paid at San Francisco, California, and at additional mailing offices. POSTMASTER: Send address changes to New Directions for Higher Education, Jossey-Bass, 989 Market Street, San Francisco, California 94103-1741.

New Directions for Higher Education is indexed in Current Index to Journals in Education (ERIC); Higher Education Abstracts.

SUBSCRIPTIONS cost $89 for individuals and $228 for institutions, agencies, and libraries. See ordering information page at end of journal.

EDITORIAL CORRESPONDENCE should be sent to the Co-Editors-in-Chief, Martin Kramer, 2807 Shasta Road, Berkeley, California 94708-2011 and Judith Block McLaughlin, Harvard GSE, Gutman 435, Cambridge, Massachusetts 02138.

Cover photograph © Digital Vision

www.josseybass.com

CONTENTS

EDITOR'S NOTES   1
Betsy O. Barefoot

1. Rethinking College Readiness   3
David T. Conley
In order to make a successful academic and social transition to college, students need to develop key cognitive strategies, content knowledge, academic behaviors, and knowledge about the college culture.

2. Blending High School and College: Rethinking the Transition   15
Nancy Hoffman, Joel Vargas, Janet Santos
A successful transition to college for increasing numbers of students requires that they begin college course work while still in high school.

3. New Challenges in Working with Traditional-Aged College Students   27
Jennifer R. Keup
As institutions and traditional-aged students change, so does the nature of student transitions to and through the first year.

4. From Helicopter Parent to Valued Partner: Shaping the Parental Relationship for Student Success   39
Marc Cutright
The role of parents in successful collegiate transition is requiring that colleges and universities find ways to communicate and collaborate with these important stakeholders.

5. Adult Students in Higher Education: A Portrait of Transitions   49
Carlette Jackson Hardin
Students who enter or reenter college as adults face their own unique challenges.

6. Sophomores in Transition: The Forgotten Year   59
Barbara F. Tobolowsky
The challenges of student transition do not end with the first year; the sophomore year includes many decision points that, if not successfully navigated, can impede or halt the progress toward degree attainment.

7. "Feeling Like a Freshman Again": The Transfer   69
Student Transition
Barbara K. Townsend
As the number of students who begin in one college and transfer to
another increases, so does the concern of campuses and state policy-
makers about this important transition experience.

8. Institutional Efforts to Move Seniors Through and   79
Beyond College
Jean M. Henscheid
The final undergraduate transition is the last opportunity for institu-
tions to ensure that students are prepared for the world beyond college.

9. College Transitions: The Other Side of the Story   89
Betsy O. Barefoot
Although many stages of collegiate transition are common for all students, the way those stages are experienced depends on students' unique
characteristics and distinctive paths through college.

INDEX   93

EDITOR'S NOTES

Transitions. From the cradle to the grave, we make them with varying degrees of success and comfort. Some are predetermined by external circumstances, and others are of our own making. Some have positive consequences, and others may send us spiraling down a path we never intended. Transitions at any point in life are almost always accompanied by some mix of excitement, hope, fulfillment, anxiety, fear, and disillusionment. The transitions that happen before, after, and during the undergraduate college experience are the subject of this volume: transitions that are experienced by students (and sometimes their parents) and guided by educators.

The topic of collegiate transitions has been a primary focus of higher education literature and research over the past twenty-five years. But almost all of this attention has centered on the first year, the transition period when students are most likely to drop out of college. In spite of its importance to students and institutions, the first year is not the only significant transition period that affects student success. This volume of *New Directions for Higher Education* expands the lens to include a view of the transitions that precede and follow the traditional first year, as well as the critical junctures throughout the undergraduate years that either promote or impede student progress to degree.

Depending on the characteristics of the students, their entry points, and their subsequent decisions, the nature of the college experience will be different. But we, the authors of this volume, believe that student success from entry to degree attainment also depends in great measure on the willingness of institutions to be supportive of and accountable for student progress in, through, and ultimately out of college.

Chapter One, by David Conley, provides an overview of important research on college readiness—the knowledge, skills, and behaviors students need in order to make a successful transition to college. In Chapter Two, Nancy Hoffman, Joel Vargas, and Janet Santos review the growing number of high school and college mergers intended to increase the numbers of students who move through the educational pipeline to an associate or baccalaureate degree.

Chapters Three and Four look at traditional-aged students (the millennials) and their parents. In Chapter Three, Jennifer Keup identifies and explores four major issues affecting the collegiate experience of students who enter college directly from high school, and in Chapter Four, Marc Cutright considers their "helicopter parents" in a new light that emphasizes

the important role parents play in the success of their college-going sons and daughters.

Carlette Jackson Hardin provides a comprehensive view of adult students in Chapter Five. She offers not only a realistic picture of the challenges these students face in going to college for the first time or after years of absence, but also recommendations for college educators who want to serve this population more effectively.

In Chapter Six, Barbara Tobolowsky considers the sophomore year, another period in which students are at risk of dropout from college. Barbara Townsend explores the transfer transition experience in Chapter Seven, using as a background her qualitative research with transfer students. And Jean M. Henscheid in Chapter Eight reviews her extensive research on programs for seniors to frame her chapter on this final collegiate transition.

In Chapter Nine, I summarize the information provided throughout the volume and present an alternative view of collegiate transition that focuses on individual rather than common experiences.

I thank each of these outstanding chapter authors for their contributions to this volume. Each has taken a different perspective on a shared theme and in doing so has helped expand our collective view of transition. We are happy to dedicate this volume to the college educators who teach, support, advise, cajole, prod, comfort, and finally celebrate students as they pass through our doors and leave to contribute to their communities and our world.

Betsy O. Barefoot
Editor

BETSY O. BAREFOOT is codirector and senior scholar in the Policy Center on the First Year of College located in Brevard, North Carolina. She is also a fellow in the National Resource Center for The First-Year Experience and Students in Transition at the University of South Carolina.

NEW DIRECTIONS FOR HIGHER EDUCATION • DOI: 10.1002/he

1

Students vary in the degree to which high school and family life prepare them for college, and that preparation has a dramatic impact on their transition to college and subsequent success there.

Rethinking College Readiness

David T. Conley

The likelihood that students will make a successful transition to the college environment is often a function of their readiness—the degree to which previous educational and personal experiences have equipped them for the expectations and demands they will encounter in college. A key problem is that the current measures of college preparation are limited in their ability to communicate to students and educators the true range of what students must do to be fully ready to succeed in college. This chapter presents a broader, more comprehensive conception of college readiness built on four facets: key cognitive strategies, key content knowledge, academic behaviors, and contextual skills and knowledge.

Recent research has shed light on the key elements of college success. At the heart of college readiness is development of the cognitive and metacognitive capabilities of incoming students: analysis, interpretation, precision and accuracy, problem solving, and reasoning. Student facility with these strategies has been consistently and emphatically identified by those who teach entry-level college courses as being centrally important to college success (Conley, 2003b, 2005; Conley and Bowers, 2008; National Research Council, 2002).

Close behind in importance is an understanding of specific types of content knowledge. Several studies have led to college readiness standards that specify key content knowledge associated with college success (Achieve, the Education Trust, and Thomas B. Fordham Foundation, 2004; ACT, 2004; College Board, 2006; Conley, 2003a, 2003b; Texas Higher

This chapter was adapted from: Conley, D. T. *Toward a Comprehensive Conception of College Readiness.* Eugene, Ore.: Educational Policy Improvement Center, 2007.

Education Coordinating Board, 2008). Writing may be the single overarching academic skill most closely associated with college success, but the major theories and concepts related to each content area are important foundational elements in their own right.

Also contributing to student success is a set of academic self-management behaviors. Among these are time management, strategic study skills, awareness of one's true performance, persistence, and the ability to use study groups. All require students to demonstrate high degrees of self-awareness, self-control, and intentionality.

Finally, an increasing number of studies have highlighted the complexity of the contextual knowledge associated with application and acculturation to college (Conley, 2005; Lundell, Higbee, Hipp, and Copeland, 2004; Venezia, Kirst, and Antonio, 2004). The application process includes a great deal of technical information, such as how to apply to college, the differences among colleges and how to choose the right college, and the intricacies of the financial aid system. The first-year college experience itself has a strong cultural component. Some students will be far more comfortable than others in this new cultural milieu, but all will experience some degree of culture shock. This contextual awareness, or "college knowledge," is necessary for students to know how to interact with professors and peers and how to participate successfully as a member of an intellectual community.

General Elements of a More Comprehensive Definition of College Readiness

College readiness can be defined as the level of preparation a student needs in order to enroll and succeed, without remediation, in a credit-bearing general education course at a postsecondary institution that offers a baccalaureate degree or transfer to a baccalaureate program. *Succeed* is defined as completing entry-level courses at a level of understanding and proficiency that makes it possible for the student to consider taking the next course in the sequence or the next level of course in the subject area.

The college-ready student envisioned by this definition is able to understand what is expected in a college course, can cope with the content knowledge that is presented, and can develop the key intellectual lessons and dispositions the course is designed to convey. In addition, the student who is ready for college will be able to understand the culture and structure of postsecondary education and the ways of knowing and intellectual norms of this academic and social environment.

How College Is Different from High School

Although the numbers of nontraditional first-year students continue to increase, the vast majority of students in their first year of college are recent high school graduates (National Center for Education Statistics, 2008) and are influenced, for better or worse, by their high school experiences. College is different from high school in many important ways—some obvious, some not so obvious. College is the first place where we expect young people to be adults, not large children. The pupil-teacher relationship changes dramatically, as do expectations for engagement, independent work, motivation, and intellectual development. All of this occurs when, for the first time, many young people are experiencing significant independence from family and from the role of child. It is no wonder that the transition from high school to college is one of the most difficult that many people experience during their lifetime.

Because college is truly different from high school, college readiness is fundamentally different from high school completion. Detailed analyses of college courses reveal that although a college course may have the same name as a high school course, college instructors pace their courses more rapidly, emphasize different aspects of the material taught, and have very different goals for their courses than do high school instructors (Conley, Aspengren, Stout, and Veach, 2006). The college instructor is more likely to expect students to make inferences, interpret results, analyze conflicting explanations of phenomena, support arguments with evidence, solve complex problems that have no obvious answer, reach conclusions, offer explanations, conduct research, engage in the give-and-take of ideas, and generally think deeply about what they are being taught (National Research Council, 2002).

Research findings describe college courses that require students to read eight to ten books in the same time that a high school class requires only one or two (Standards for Success, 2003). In college classes, students write multiple papers in rapid succession (National Survey of Student Engagement, 2003, 2004, 2006). These papers should be well reasoned, well organized, and well supported with evidence from credible sources. By contrast, high school students may write one or two research papers at most throughout all of high school and may take weeks or months to do so. Increasingly, college courses in all subject areas require research capabilities, the ability to read and comprehend a wide array of document types, and well-developed writing skills.

Contrary to popular misconception, most first-year college students work in groups inside and outside class on complex problems and projects and make class presentations. They are not simply lectured to. At the same time, they are expected to be independent, self-reliant learners who recognize when they are having problems and know when and how to seek help from professors, students, or other sources. College faculty also report that first-year students need to be spending nearly twice the time they indicate they spend currently to prepare for class (National Survey of Student Engagement, 2006).

Finally, the relationship between teacher and student can be much different than it was in high school. An oft-cited example by college faculty is the first-term first-year student who is failing a course and sends an e-mail near the end of the term without ever having communicated with the professor previously requesting "extra credit" in order to be able to pass. Students complain bitterly when no special arrangements are forthcoming.

In short, the differences in expectations between high school and college are manifold and significant. To be successful in college, students must be prepared to use an array of learning strategies and coping skills that are quite different from those they developed and honed in high school.

Components in a Comprehensive Definition of College Readiness

College readiness is a multifaceted concept comprising numerous factors internal and external to the classroom environment. The model presented in Figure 1.1 derives from my research and organizes the key areas necessary for college readiness into four concentric levels.

In practice, these various facets are neither mutually exclusive nor perfectly nested as portrayed in the model. They interact with one another extensively. For example, a lack of college knowledge often affects the decisions students make regarding the content knowledge they choose to study and master. Or a lack of attention to time management and study skills is one of the most frequent causes of problems for first-year students, even if they possess sufficient content knowledge.

Figure 1.1. Facets of College Readiness

The model, explained in greater detail below, argues for a more comprehensive look at what it means to be college ready and more attention to preparation that addresses all four facets.

Key Cognitive Strategies

Several studies of college faculty members nationwide, regardless of the selectivity of the university, expressed near-universal agreement that students arrive largely unprepared for the intellectual demands and expectations of postsecondary education (Conley, 2003b). They have difficulty formulating and solving problems, evaluating and incorporating reference material appropriately, developing a logical and coherent argument or explanation, interpreting data or conflicting points of view, and completing their assignments and projects with precision and accuracy (Conley, McGaughy, and Gray, 2008).

The success of a well-prepared college student is built on a foundation of key cognitive strategies that enable students to learn content from a range of disciplines:

- *Problem formulation and problem solving.* The student develops and applies multiple strategies to formulate and solve routine and nonroutine problems and selects the appropriate method for solving complex problems.
- *Research.* The student engages in active inquiry and dialogue about subject matter and research questions and seeks evidence to defend arguments, explanations, or lines of reasoning. The student documents assertions and builds an argument that extends from previous findings or arguments. The student uses appropriate references to support an assertion or a line of reasoning. The student identifies and evaluates data, material, and sources for quality of content, validity, credibility, and relevance. The student compares and contrasts sources and findings and generates summaries and explanations of source materials.
- *Reasoning, argumentation, and proof.* The student constructs well-reasoned arguments or proofs to explain phenomena or issues, uses recognized forms of reasoning to construct an argument and defend a point of view or conclusion, accepts critiques of or challenge to assertions, and addresses critiques and challenges by providing a logical explanation or refutation or by acknowledging the accuracy of the critique or challenge.
- *Interpretation.* The student analyzes competing and conflicting descriptions of an event or issue to determine the strengths and flaws in each description and any commonalities among or distinctions between them. The student synthesizes the results of an analysis of competing or conflicting descriptions of an event, issue, or phenomenon into a coherent explanation. The student states the interpretation that is most likely correct or is most reasonable based on the available evidence. The student presents orally or in writing an extended description, summary, and evaluation of varied perspectives and conflicting points of view on a topic or issue.

• *Precision and accuracy.* The student knows what type of precision is appropriate to the task and the subject area, is able to increase precision and accuracy when a task or process is repeated, and uses precision appropriately to reach correct conclusions in the context of the task or subject.

These key cognitive strategies are broadly representative of the foundational elements that underlie various ways of knowing. They are at the heart of the intellectual endeavor of the university and necessary to discern truth and meaning, as well as to pursue them. They are also at the heart of how postsecondary faculty members think about their subject areas.

Academic Knowledge and Skills

Following are some of the key structures, concepts, and knowledge associated with core academic subjects. A more comprehensive exposition is presented in *College Knowledge* (Conley, 2005).

English. The knowledge and skills developed in entry-level English courses enable students to engage texts critically and create well-written, well-organized, and well-supported products, both oral and written. The foundations of English include reading comprehension, literature, writing, editing, information gathering, analysis, critiques, and connections. To be ready to succeed in such courses, students need to build vocabulary and word analysis skills. Similarly, they need to use techniques such as strategic reading that will help them understand a wide range of nonfiction and technical texts. Knowing how to slow down to understand key points, when to reread a passage, and how to underline key terms and concepts strategically so that only the most important points are highlighted aids comprehension and retention of key content.

Math. Students with a thorough understanding of the basic concepts, principles, and techniques of algebra are more likely to succeed in an entry-level college mathematics course. College-ready students possess more than a formulaic understanding of mathematics. They have the ability to apply conceptual understandings in order to extract a problem from a context, solve the problem, and interpret the solution back into the context. They know when and how to estimate to determine the reasonableness of answers and can use a calculator appropriately as a tool, not a crutch.

Science. College science courses emphasize scientific thinking in all its facets. In addition to using all the steps in the scientific method, students learn what it means to think like a scientist. This includes the communication conventions that scientists follow, the way that empirical evidence is used to draw conclusions, and how such conclusions are then subject to challenge and interpretation. Students come to appreciate that scientific knowledge is both constant and changing at any given moment and that the evolution of scientific knowledge does not mean that previous knowledge

NEW DIRECTIONS FOR HIGHER EDUCATION • DOI: 10.1002/he

was necessarily wrong. Students grasp that scientists think in terms of models and systems as ways to comprehend complex phenomena. They master core concepts, principles, laws, and vocabulary of the scientific discipline being studied. Laboratory settings are the environments where content knowledge and scientific thinking strategies converge to help students comprehend content knowledge fully.

Social Studies. The social sciences entail a range of subject areas, each with its own content base, analytical techniques, and conventions. The analytical methods that are common across the social studies emphasize the skills of interpreting sources, evaluating evidence and competing claims, and understanding themes and events within larger frameworks. Helping students be aware that the social sciences consist of theories and concepts that are used to order and structure all of the overwhelming detail can help them build mental scaffolds that lead toward thinking like a social scientist.

World Languages. The goal of second-language study is to communicate effectively with and receive communication from speakers of another language in authentic cultural contexts. Learning another language involves much more than memorizing a system of grammatical rules. It requires the learner to understand the cultures from which the language arises and in which it resides, use the language to communicate accurately, and use the learner's first language and culture as a model for comparison with the second language. Language learners need to understand the structure and conventions of a language, and not solely or primarily through word-for-word translation or memorization of decontextualized grammatical rules. Instead, students of a language need to master meaning in more holistic and contextual ways.

Arts. The arts encompass art history, dance, music, theater, and the visual arts. Students ready for college-level work in these subjects possess an understanding of and appreciation for the contributions made by the most innovative creators in the field. Students think of themselves as instruments of communication and expression who demonstrate mastery of basic oral and physical expression through sound, movement, and visual representations. They understand the role of the arts as an instrument of social and political expression. They are able to justify their aesthetic decisions when creating or performing a piece of work and know how to make decisions regarding the proper venue for performing or exhibiting any creative product.

Academic Behaviors

This facet of college readiness encompasses behaviors that reflect greater student self-awareness, self-monitoring, and self-control of processes and actions necessary for academic success. These tend to transcend content areas.

Self-management is a form of metacognition—the act of thinking about how one is thinking. Research on the thinking of effective learners has shown that such individuals tend to monitor actively, regulate, evaluate, and direct their own thinking (Ritchhart, 2002). Examples of some key self-management skill areas are awareness of one's current level of mastery and understanding (and misunderstandings) of a subject; the ability to reflect on what worked and what needed improvement regarding a particular academic task; the ability to persist when presented with a novel, difficult, or ambiguous task; the tendency to identify and systematically select among and employ a range of learning strategies; and the capability to transfer learning and strategies from familiar settings and situations to new ones (Bransford, Brown, and Cocking, 2000).

Another important set of academic behaviors is student mastery of study skills necessary for college success. College courses require that significant amounts of time be devoted to out-of-class study. Study skills encompass active learning strategies that go far beyond reading the text and answering the homework questions.

Important study-skill behaviors include time management, stress management, task prioritizing, using information resources, taking class notes, and communicating with teachers and advisers (Robbins and others, 2004). An additional critical skill is the ability to participate successfully in a study group and recognize its potential value.

Time management is perhaps the most foundational of all the self-management and study skills. Examples of time management techniques and habits include accurately estimating how much time it takes to complete outstanding and anticipated tasks and allocating sufficient time to complete the tasks, using calendars and creating to-do lists to organize studying into productive chunks of time, locating and using settings conducive to proper study, and prioritizing study time in relation to competing demands such as work and socializing.

Contextual Skills and Awareness

College knowledge, that is, contextual skills and awareness, is the information students need to apply successfully to college, gain necessary financial aid, and then, subsequent to matriculation, understand how college operates as a system and culture.

The first dimension of college knowledge is the information—both formal and informal, stated and unstated—necessary to be eligible for admission, select an appropriate postsecondary institution, gain admission to a college, and obtain financial aid. Students with college knowledge understand college admission criteria including high school course requirements, know how to complete an application, understand that different colleges have different missions, can state approximate tuition costs and the likelihood of financial aid from various types of colleges, and know admissions-testing requirements and deadlines (Conley, 2005; Robbins and others, 2004; Venezia, Kirst, and Antonio, 2004).

College knowledge is distributed inequitably in society, and the lack of it frustrates and discourages many students who are the first in their families to attend college. They may miss one of the myriad deadlines or overlook potential financial aid. Some of them simply do not apply at all. Many first-generation students who do attend struggle to become successful participants in the campus community; become alienated, frustrated, and even humiliated during the first year; and leave college precipitously.

Success in college is enhanced for students who possess the knowledge and skills that enable them to interact with a diverse cross-section of academicians and peers. These include the ability to collaborate and work on a team; knowledge of the norms of the academic culture and how to interact with professors, administrators, and others in that environment; the ability to be comfortable around people from different backgrounds and cultures; the ability to take advantage of academic and personal support resources available on most campuses; and the ability to demonstrate leadership skills in a variety of settings.

Conclusion

Clearly, far fewer students are truly ready for college when measured against this multidimensional model than when judged by the conventional standard of courses taken and grades received in high school. The goal of presenting a more comprehensive model of college readiness is not to deny students entrance to college but to highlight the gaps that exist between those who are college eligible and those who are college ready.

Colleges can take steps to ensure that more students are college ready. First, they should adopt a set of college readiness standards that affirm the importance of the key cognitive strategies and content knowledge incoming students need to know. At the very least, students should have an honest idea if they are adequately prepared for entry-level college courses. Parents should also know this. Ideally colleges will work with feeder high schools to create scoring guides, assignments, and even courses that help students diagnose their level of preparation for college in the key areas identified in this chapter. Every entry-level general education course can easily specify the key cognitive strategies and content knowledge that will be developed in the course and where students can go for help if they are concerned about their capabilities in a particular area.

Second, although an ideal K-16 educational system would eliminate the need for remedial (developmental) education, when such programs are necessary, they should be clearly focused on enabling students to grasp the key cognitive strategies, key content knowledge, and self-management skills necessary for college success. They should not simply focus on basic skills and ignore important thinking skills, key concepts of the core disciplines, and the structure of these subject areas. Colleges need better diagnostic information on incoming students in order to tailor remedial programs more closely to individual student needs and prepare them better for what they will encounter in entry-level courses.

Third, colleges that want to retain more first-generation attenders need to simplify the application and financial aid processes and provide better support services for these students. Assigning a personal mentor to each first-generation attender is one strategy to help these students develop college knowledge. The college can organize events at which these students learn to appreciate and enjoy academic culture while they also have an opportunity to express concerns and solve problems. Colleges can also work closely with feeder high schools to introduce collegiate culture and demystify college for high school students.

By adopting the four-part conception of college readiness presented in this chapter, high schools and colleges can use the same language to communicate what it takes for students to be ready for postsecondary education. The advantages and importance of greater agreement on what constitutes college readiness are apparent at a time when an ever-increasing proportion of high school students are choosing to go to college. Making certain that they are not just eligible but prepared will help students achieve their goals and help colleges function more effectively.

References

Achieve, the Education Trust, and Thomas B. Fordham Foundation. "Ready or Not: Creating a High School Diploma That Counts." 2004. Retrieved Apr. 10, 2008, from http://www.achieve.org/files/ADPreport_7.pdf.

ACT. "On Course for Success: A Close Look at Selected High School Courses That Prepare All Students for College." 2004. Retrieved Apr. 10, 2008, from http://www.act.org/research/policymakers/pdf/success_report.pdf.

Bransford, J. D., Brown, A. L., and Cocking, R. R. (eds.). *How People Learn: Brain, Mind, Experience, and School.* Washington, D.C.: National Academy of Sciences, 2000.

College Board. *Standards for College Success.* New York: College Board, 2006.

Conley, D. T. *Mixed Messages: What State High School Tests Communicate About Student Readiness for College.* Eugene, Ore.: Center for Educational Policy Research, University of Oregon, 2003a.

Conley, D. T. *Understanding University Success.* Eugene, Ore.: Center for Educational Policy Research, University of Oregon, 2003b.

Conley, D. T. *College Knowledge: What It Really Takes for Students to Succeed and What We Can Do to Get Them Ready.* San Francisco: Jossey-Bass, 2005.

Conley, D. T., Aspengren, K., Stout, O., and Veach, D. *College Board Advanced Placement Best Practices Course Study Report.* Eugene, Ore.: Educational Policy Improvement Center, 2006.

Conley, D. T., and Bowers, C. J. "Analyzing Science Course Content: Implications for Instruction and System Alignment." Paper presented at the meeting of the American Educational Research Association, New York, Mar. 26, 2008.

Conley, D. T., McGaughy, C., and Gray, E. *College Readiness Performance Assessment System.* Eugene, Ore.: Educational Policy Improvement Center, 2008.

Lundell, D. B., Higbee, J. L., Hipp, S., and Copeland, R. E. *Building Bridges for Access and Success from High School to College: Proceedings of the Metropolitan Higher Education Consortium's Developmental Education Initiative.* Minneapolis: Center for Research on Developmental Education and Urban Literacy, University of Minnesota, 2004.

National Center for Education Statistics. "Postsecondary Fast Facts," 2008. Retrieved Apr. 28, 2008, from http://nces.ed.gov/fastfacts/display.asp?id=98.

National Research Council. *Learning and Understanding: Improving Advanced Study of Mathematics and Science in U.S. High Schools.* Washington, D.C.: National Academy Press, 2002.

National Survey of Student Engagement. "Converting Data into Action: Expanding the Boundaries of Institutional Improvement." 2003. Retrieved Oct. 19, 2004, from.http://nsse.iub.edu/2003_annual_report/pdf/NSSE_2003_annual_report.pdf.

National Survey of Student Engagement. "Student Engagement: Pathways to Student Success." 2004. Retrieved Jan. 18, 2005, from http://nsse.iub.edu/2004_annual_report/pdf/annual_report.pdf.

National Survey of Student Engagement. *Engaged Learning: Fostering Success for All Students.* Bloomington, Ind.: National Survey of Student Engagement, 2006.

Ritchhart, R. *Intellectual Character: What It Is, Why It Matters, and How to Get It.* San Francisco: Jossey-Bass, 2002.

Robbins, S. B., and others. "Do Psychosocial and Study Skill Factors Predict College Outcomes? A Meta-Analysis." *Psychological Bulletin,* 2004, *130,* 261–288.

Standards for Success. *An Introduction to Work Samples and Their Uses.* Eugene: Center for Educational Policy Research, University of Oregon, 2003.

Texas Higher Education Coordinating Board. *College Readiness Standards.* Austin: Texas Higher Education Coordinating Board, 2008.

Venezia, A., Kirst, M., and Antonio, A. *Betraying the College Dream: How Disconnected K-12 and Postsecondary Systems Undermine Student Aspirations.* San Francisco: Jossey-Bass, 2004.

DAVID T. CONLEY is professor of educational policy and leadership in the College of Education, University of Oregon. He is the founder and director of the Center for Educational Policy Research at the University of Oregon.

NEW DIRECTIONS FOR HIGHER EDUCATION • DOI: 10.1002/he

2

For many students the first year of college begins before high school ends. This reality is requiring that educators rethink their traditional notions of the first year.

Blending High School and College: Rethinking the Transition

Nancy Hoffman, Joel Vargas, Janet Santos

If everyone needs an education through two years of college or the equivalent, then the nation has an obligation to provide a far more certain pathway for postsecondary success than it does now. Because so many young people fail to complete the final years of high school, graduate but do not apply to college, or begin postsecondary education only to drop out within the first few semesters, the transition years from high school to college take on great importance in increasing the degree attainment rates of U.S. young people. In the years between grades 9 and 14, young people are most vulnerable to the educational failure that will severely limit their life chances.

Our current K-16 system is a study in contrasts—economic and racial/ethnic contrasts that are unhealthy for the United States. Nationally, young people from middle- and upper-income families are five times more likely to earn a two- or four-year college degree than those from low-income families. Only 11 percent of the low-income students who were eighth graders in 2001 are projected to earn a college degree by 2014 compared with 52 percent of their more affluent peers (Goldberger, 2007).

Several leaks along the educational pipeline account for this huge disparity, beginning with the high school experience:

- Only 65 percent of low-income students complete high school, compared with 91 percent of their middle- and upper-income peers.
- Only 22 percent of low-income students graduate from high school academically prepared for college, compared with 54 percent of middle- and upper-income students.

NEW DIRECTIONS FOR HIGHER EDUCATION, no. 144, Winter 2008   © Wiley Periodicals, Inc.
Published online in Wiley InterScience (www.interscience.wiley.com) • DOI: 10.1002/he.322

15

- Only 42 percent of low-income youth who graduate from high school prepared for college go on to earn a degree, compared with 73 percent of similarly prepared middle- and upper-income high school graduates (Goldberger, 2007).

Such data call for radical interventions to increase the number of low-income young people gaining postsecondary credentials.

There are a number of ways to increase high school graduation rates and put more students on the path to and through college. One strategy for ensuring that more students will complete high school and earn a postsecondary credential is to provide young people the option to do college-level work in high school. These accelerated learning options can serve as an on-ramp to college for underprepared students and a fast track for those already college bound. Approaches serving the former group are the subject discussed in this chapter.

First, we describe three accelerated learning options: traditional dual enrollment, dual enrollment pathways, and early college schools. We then present minicases of the latter two options, discuss the responses of young people to these new opportunities, and briefly review the evidence that such options can do what they claim: increase college success. Finally, we summarize some lessons learned by Jobs for the Future, our organization, about this work.

Accelerated Learning Options

The three accelerated learning options we examine are traditional dual enrollment, dual enrollment pathways, and early college schools.

Dual Enrollment. Dual enrollment programs allow students to enroll in college-level course work and earn credit for it while they are still in high school. Students typically enroll in college courses in their junior and senior years. In most programs, courses result in dual credit: the college course replaces a required high school course, and the student earns credit for both. In some programs, however, students must choose between high school and college credit. Most dual enrollment programs offer free or discounted tuition, providing some savings for families who otherwise might not be able to afford sending their children to college.

Dual enrollment is also called *dual credit, concurrent enrollment, college in the high school,* and *joint enrollment.* These terms typically refer to high school students' taking college courses on either the high school or college campus. Any of these program variations can fall under the umbrella of what some states call postsecondary or accelerated learning options.

One data point exemplifies the potential of accelerated learning options to increase the likelihood that students currently underrepresented in higher education will succeed in postsecondary education. *The Tool Box Revisited* (Adelman, 2006), a study by the U.S. Department of Education, indicates that the accumulation of twenty college credits by the end of the first calendar year of college is a strong predictor that a student will earn a college credential. If the accelerated high school program is intensive—that is, if students gain twenty or more credits—it is our estimation that such credit attainment should also be highly correlated with the student's likelihood of earning a postsecondary credential. In addition, such credit attainment is certainly a strong indicator that the student is ready for college.

While participation in dual enrollment programs has existed for several decades, some states have made changes in the purpose, structure, and visibility of these programs in the past five years, moving them from their sole use as an escape from high school for advanced students and reconceiving them as an effective route to college and technical education for a wide range of students. In this new configuration, dual enrollment becomes a central strategy for increasing college-going rates of high school students, and the expectation is that students will receive help in course selection and academic support as needed.

Dual enrollment has another advantage in making college access more equitable. In rural and low-income areas, where advanced courses may not be available to high school students, accelerated learning options may be provided virtually or by high school teachers or adjuncts certified by a college. For these reasons, a number of states are making the opportunity to earn college credit in high school available to every high school student in the state.

Dual Enrollment Pathways. A second structure for dual enrollment, and one for which there is not yet settled terminology, is what we call *dual enrollment pathways*. Within a traditional high school, students participate in a preselected sequence of college courses (two to four courses), sometimes preceded by a "college 101" introduction to study skills. The pathway includes opportunities for those not likely to qualify for college admission without remediation—students who are at risk of graduating with weak preparation for college—to become qualified. In addition, such enhanced programs often reach out to middle school students, familiarizing them with the demands of postsecondary education and the environment on a college campus.

In dual enrollment pathways, courses are carefully chosen to meet postsecondary career certificate or general education requirements in two-year institutions and to be transferable. The expectation is that students will require and receive substantial academic support and that taxpayers will receive a return on this investment as more young people enter the labor market with a credential, contribute to the state's economy, and pay taxes.

In terms of scale, dual enrollment pathways are not as prevalent as traditional dual enrollment. To qualify as a true dual enrollment pathway, students would graduate from high school with anywhere from one to four semesters of college credit. These programs are in early stages of development and thus not widely known, but interesting models already exist. With over thirty thousand enrollments in college courses by high school students in 2004–2005, the City University of New York's College Now program, described later in this chapter, is the largest and most developed example of which we are aware (Meade and Hofmann, 2007). In addition, an increasing number of states have proposed providing around thirty college credits to all qualified high school students. Our assumption is that implementation will require the establishment of pathways.

Early College Schools. While also relatively small in scale, the third accelerated option, early college schools, is quickly garnering considerable attention nationally. Early college schools currently serve over fifteen thousand underrepresented students in small, autonomous schools, and the number already funded and planned will reach over ninety-five thousand students by 2012. Like dual enrollment pathways, they align and integrate course sequences across the sectors with the goal of promoting postsecondary completion. Early college schools are designed so that students underrepresented in postsecondary education (low-income students, student of color, and first-generation college students) can simultaneously earn a high school diploma and an associate degree or up to two years of credit toward a bachelor's degree, and earn it tuition free. Each school is developed in partnership with a postsecondary institution whose courses make up the college portion of the students' education. Students begin college-level work as early as ninth grade, often with a "college 101" seminar.

Early college schools have three designs: grade 6–12 schools that incorporate two years of college within the same time that a student would take to complete a high school diploma; four-year programs that incorporate up to thirty college credits by the end of twelfth grade; and five-year programs that start in ninth grade and incorporate up to sixty college credits by the end of the fifth year. The fifth year takes place entirely on a college campus.

Requirements for a Successful Transition

For young people to make a successful transition into postsecondary education and get on a secure path to attaining a credential, three resources are essential and must exist across grades 9 through 14: a rigorous academic program that sequences and scaffolds academic demands in a trajectory that moves without break from high school through college-level work; dependable financing for higher education promised at least by ninth grade; and a web of support—school-based, familial, and community—through high school and into postsecondary education.

In regard to the first requirement—a rigorous academic program that moves without break from high school through college-level work—increasing numbers and more varied students across the country are taking part in accelerated learning options that provide college-level credit during high school. In some states, as many as 20 percent of high school students graduate with college credit (Hoffman, 2005). All such options raise the academic stakes for young people, providing them with academic challenges beyond what their high schools offer. In varying degrees of intensity, all introduce students to college academic expectations, and those models in which students take a sequence of courses approach the goal of seamlessness in the transition to postsecondary education.

As for financing, most accelerated learning options provide transferable college credit free of charge, and some result in as much as two years of tuition-free college credit in high school. Not only do such programs motivate students because they save money for their families, they also signal that educators believe so strongly in the need for all young people to attain a postsecondary credential that they are willing to invest public dollars.

Dual Enrollment Pathways Example

New York State has no dual enrollment legislation, but the City University of New York and the New York Department of Education, the largest urban postsecondary system and the largest urban school district in the country, respectively, have established an extensive high school–postsecondary partnership. Led by City University of New York (CUNY), College Now is widely recognized as a national model for an integrated K-16 system.

College Now's mission is to help students meet high school graduation and college entrance requirements without remediation and to be retained through a degree. Begun in 1984 at Kingsborough Community College, College Now expanded in 1999 when the CUNY board voted to end remediation at CUNY's senior colleges. The program was designed specifically to serve students who might not otherwise be able to attend postsecondary institutions and who receive inadequate college preparation in the city's high schools. Most CUNY students are poor (the average family income is twenty-eight thousand dollars), most work, and retention and graduation rates are low, even at six years from college entry (Tracy Meade, personal communication to Janet Santos, January 14, 2008).

The centerpiece of College Now is its free, credit-bearing college courses. College Now differs from most other dual enrollment options in that courses are offered not at random, but in a structured sequence or pathway with academic supports as needed. All credits are transferable within the CUNY system, but college courses do not replace high school courses.

There is very little empirical research on the impact of dual enrollment on student persistence and achievement, and even less on student development. But because of the scope of College Now and its high visibility as a bridge to college for public school students in the nation's largest school district, it has attracted the attention of researchers. Melinda Mechur Karp, a senior research associate at the Institute on Education and the Economy/Community College Research Center at Columbia University, wrote her dissertation on identity development among College Now students (Karp, 2006) and has focused her research on dual enrollment and credit-based transition programs across the nation. Karp was interested in understanding whether

dual enrollment programs like College Now encourage student matriculation and persistence in college. She hypothesized that these programs provide students with an opportunity to try on the role of college student,
thereby increasing their understanding of the role. Once matriculated in college, they would not feel "strange." Karp (2006) argues:

> Presumably, students who are familiar with the demands of postsecondary
> education and are able to successfully meet those demands are likely to
> matriculate into and persist in college. If dual enrollment is shown to help
> students learn what it means to "be a college student," policymakers may
> have reason to believe that widespread participation in dual enrollment
> may lead to increased college access and success [p. 5].

Karp (2006) carried out in-depth interviews with twenty-six students from
backgrounds typical of the CUNY system over the course of the first semester in which they were dually enrolled. All were taking only one college
course, which was taught in their high schools, not on the college
campus. Thus, the impact on the students' understanding of the college student role and any changes in their identities depended on the single course
experience, not on a sequence of courses or experiencing the college campus environment or being in class with regular college students.

Karp (2006) concluded that eighteen students "shifted their conceptions
of the college student role over the course of the semester," and a smaller
number "began to integrate the college student role into their self-concepts"
(p. 80). Not surprisingly, she observed that the more college-like the courses
were in structure, demands, and presentation, the greater the shift was in students' sense of themselves as college students. For example, in Karp's terms,
the English and psychology courses had the greatest "authenticity" and were
of highest quality, and these courses allowed students the greatest opportunities to "rehearse" the college student role (p. 80).

Because underprepared students so often are confounded by the rules
of the game even more than by the intellectual demands in their first year of
college, Karp's qualitative study (2006) asks important questions. As she
notes, students who were in well-implemented, high-quality dual enrollment courses "were able to articulate the demands of the role more clearly,
more strategically, and with greater depth of understanding at the end of the
semester than they were at the beginning" (p. 80).

For her dissertation, Karp held periodic interviews with "Saily." Karp
(2006) reports that in March 2004, when first asked to describe "a typical
college student," Saily replied, "I don't know exactly what a typical college student is like, 'cause I haven't gone to college and I don't know many people who
are in college." By her third interview with Saily in June 2004, Karp reports:

> [She] went into great detail, offering a general description of college students'
> behaviors and attitudes, as well as strategies that college students might use

to successfully enact the role. She understood that college students must take responsibility for their academic progress, and must balance newfound freedom (both academic and personal) with school demands. In class, college students often engage in discussions, and Saily recognized that these discussions require them to be open-minded. She also said that college students must be organized and skilled in time management. She described thought processes and strategies that college students use to accomplish this by saying: "you have to like state out what you are gonna do like Tuesday and Wednesday and Thursday. I have to get my projects for this class and then I have to read for this class on that day so I could be prepared and stuff. You have to give yourself like an outline for the week" [p. 54].

One of the questions that states and institutions are asking about dual enrollment is how many and what kind of college courses in high school provide the amount of college needed to ensure persistence and degree attainment. Karp's data suggest that even a single authentic college course can help first-generation urban students like those in New York City onto a path toward college.

There are also positive outcomes from quantitative, large-scale studies of College Now. One study suggests that College Now puts students on a path toward college completion (Michalowski, 2006). Among first-time freshmen, participants were more likely on average to enroll for a third semester and on average had higher grade point averages than their classmates with no College Now experience. They also earned more credit on average than nonparticipants by the end of their first year.

A second large-scale quantitative analysis, by Karp and others (2007), examines dual enrollment outcomes in New York and Florida. This study, which used the few longitudinal data sets currently available, had additional promising findings, among them that dual enrollment was positively related to enrollment in college for both the full sample (Florida) and students in New York vocational high schools who participated in College Now. College course taking also corresponded to higher enrollment in a four-year institution and had positive effects on retention and grade point average. Strikingly, dual enrollment students had earned 15.1 more credits than their peers who were not in dual enrollment three years after high school graduation (Karp and others, 2007).

Early College High Schools Examples

Over the past four years, Michael Nakkula and Karen Foster (2007), specialists in the psychosocial development of at-risk adolescents, regularly interviewed students, teachers, advisers, and parents from the Wallis Annenberg High School and Dayton Early College Academy, two schools in the early college network, to understand the ways in which students experience the college-going opportunities presented to them.

New Directions for Higher Education • DOI: 10.1002/he

The Wallis Annenberg High School in Los Angeles is part of a charter school from preschool to grade 12 that preceded the establishment of the early college high school. Located in the heart of South Central Los Angeles, it serves a largely Mexican American and African American student population. The school's higher education partner is California State University, Los Angeles. Now in its fifth year as an early college, Wallis Annenberg provides its high school students with college courses during the summer on campus and in the high school during the year. For example, in the summer of 2006, after their junior year, approximately sixty students completed courses at the college in economics, history, and critical thinking.

The Dayton Early College Academy (DECA) in Ohio is adjacent to the campus of its higher education partner, the University of Dayton. A private Catholic institution serving an affluent white population, University of Dayton was in part attracted to the idea of supporting a school in order to bring greater racial, ethnic, and income diversity to the campus. DECA students are primarily African American and low income. DECA was started by and is most strongly affiliated with the university's School of Education and Allied Professions. Since DECA's inception, the higher-education partnership has expanded to include Sinclair Community College, where many early college high school students take courses toward an associate degree.

Nakkula and Foster (2007) were particularly interested in what they call educational identity development: how students come to see themselves as learners and the impact of such self-perceptions on their views of the future, particularly on their ongoing education and career development. Nakkula and Foster believe that the transition to postsecondary education can be demoralizing and humiliating for students coming from under-resourced and underperforming high schools. Their research over many years tells them that most students have the intelligence to catch up, but psychological factors often stand in the way.

They wanted to know if early colleges where "college *expectations*, college *exposure and experience*, and college-level *challenges*" are "scaffolded through advisor and teacher support," and where the transition to postsecondary work is built into the curriculum could make a difference for students of color and low-income students who are average in academic aptitude and often underachieving (Nakkula and Foster, 2007, p. 153). They recognized the double standard, as does the early college initiative: that average middle- and upper-income students are expected to attend and complete college, while it is an expectation primarily for only exceptional low-income students and students of color.

Nakkula and Foster (2007) note that "college expectations are communicated in every facet of the early college high school experience, from application and placement interview, through ninth-grade orientation" (p. 153) and later through high school college-related advising. And leaders from both schools are clear that success must be defined by students' ability to perform adequately in nonremedial college courses while still in high school, along with the usual high school assessments. As these researchers and others note, college awareness experiences such as information on and discussion of the college application process, admissions, and financial aid have their impact on students. But two additional factors, unique to early college, by far outweigh the others in their impact on academic identity development: the location of the schools on or adjacent to the college campus and the ability to pass college courses.

In regard to location on or near a campus, the researchers noted that by the end of the ninth grade, DECA students already spoke of "feeling like a college student," and "they attributed this feeling to being a part of the college campus, including using the dining areas, classrooms, and the gymnasium" (p. 153). As for college courses, most early college students are taking these by the eleventh grade at the latest, although many start in ninth grade. (In the CUNY-related early colleges, which start in sixth grade, students are taking college minicourses on a college campus with actual college professors by seventh grade.) Preparation for college courses includes much that is taught in strong suburban high schools: developing library research strategies, revising and resubmitting work, using a calendar to set deadlines for assignments, and learning how to take notes on a lecture. But it is success itself in college course work that shapes students' emerging view of themselves as learners and future college students. Core knowledge derived from early college high schools includes knowing that one can succeed in college. As Nakkula and Foster point out, "Knowing is different from believing. Knowing . . . is rooted in experiential evidence. Whereas believing is largely an abstract, future-oriented phenomenon—'I believe I can succeed in college, based on my success in high school'—knowing has a stronger, immediately relevant, experiential foundation: 'I know I can succeed in college because I have begun to do it'" (p. 155).

Five years into the early college initiatives, data on college course taking are beginning to emerge as more and more early college students reach eleventh and twelfth grades, where they are predominantly in college courses in their schools' partner institutions. In 2007, more than nine hundred students graduated from seventeen early college high schools around the country. Their achievements far surpass those of their peers from traditional high schools serving similar populations.

Perhaps the most robust early evidence comes from North Carolina. Since 2004, North Carolina has opened forty-two early colleges, known in the state as Learn & Earn schools. These currently serve about fifty-one hundred students, and the state plans to open thirty-three more (Geoff Coltrane, personal communication to Joel Vargas, January 15, 2008). Learn & Earn schools support students to earn up to two years of college credit or an associate degree, along with a high school diploma within five years, free of charge. Students are reflective of local school district populations, and Learn & Earn particularly targets students not normally found on a college path. In the first randomized study of early college results in North Carolina, the results from a small pilot are positive: "Nearly twice as many students at Rutherford Early College High School in 2005–06 had successfully completed college preparatory mathematics courses by the end of 9th grade as compared to their peers who were not randomly selected to attend the school" (North Carolina General Assembly, 2008, p. 5).

In 2007–2008, North Carolina invested $15.2 million in Learn & Earn. Starting in 2007, it also made college courses available at no cost to any North Carolina high school student over the Internet through Learn & Earn On-Line.

Lessons Learned: Practice and Policy

In order to make a successful transition to postsecondary education, young people need a rigorous academic program, dependable financing for higher education, and a web of support—school based, familial, and community— through high school and into postsecondary institutions. The accelerated learning options we have described address the first of these: by blending high school and college-level work, these options raise the academic stakes for young people. In early colleges, students may not even experience the moment of transition to college because the college has been their "home" since seventh or ninth grade and their first year is well under way or complete by the time they matriculate. Early colleges and some dual enrollment pathways also do well at providing social, psychological, and financial support. Indeed, students often cite the opportunity to get "free" college courses as the motivator to do the hard work needed both to catch up and accelerate in high school.

Besides their impact on individual students, accelerated learning options have an impact on institutional practices, bringing colleges closer to their partner high schools. A successful accelerated learning initiative requires the following of institutions involved in a partnership:

- Formal structures that link a high school and a partner college such as a renewable partnership agreement; a person serving as liaison between high school and college; and a decision-making body to design, monitor, and collect data about the program.
- A feedback loop to high schools from postsecondary on student success. High school and college transcripts include college course grades and call attention to how well courses are sequenced between high school and college and how well high schools are preparing students for college work.
- Shared responsibility (financial and otherwise) by leaders in both secondary and postsecondary education institutions for continued collaboration.

Such partnerships can also help modify state policies so that all students succeed through and beyond the first year of college. Increasing numbers of states are now offering or considering offering free college courses to high school students as a bridge to college for underrepresented students, as well as a head start on college for those already on their way.

References

Adelman, C. *The Toolbox Revisited.* Washington, D.C.: U.S. Department of Education, 2006.

Goldberger, S. "Doing the Math: What It Means to Double the Numbers of Low-Income College Graduates." In N. Hoffman, J. Vargas, A. Venezia, and M. Miller (eds.), *Minding the Gap: Why Integrating High School with College Makes Sense and How to Do It.* Cambridge, Mass.: Harvard Education Press, 2007.

Hoffman, N. *Add and Subtract: Dual Enrollment as a State Strategy to Increase Postsecondary Success for Underrepresented Students.* Boston: Jobs for the Future, 2005.

Karp, M. "Facing the Future: Identity Development Among College Now Students." Unpublished doctoral dissertation, Columbia University, 2006.

Karp, M., and others. *The Postsecondary Achievement of Participants in Dual Enrollment: An Analysis of Student Outcomes in Two States.* New York: Community College Research Center, Teachers College, Columbia University, 2007.

Meade, T., and Hofmann, E. "CUNY College Now: Extending the Reach of Dual Enrollment." In N. Hoffman, J. Vargas, A. Venezia, and M. Miller (eds.), *Minding the Gap: Why Integrating High School with College Makes Sense and How to Do It.* Cambridge, Mass.: Harvard Education Press, 2007.

Michalowski, S. Unpublished presentation. Presented at Jobs for the Future Meeting on CUNY College Now Data, June 6, 2006.

Nakkula, M. J., and Foster, K. C. "Academic Identity Development: Student Experiences in Two Early College High Schools." In N. Hoffman, J. Vargas, A. Venezia, and M. Miller (eds.), *Minding the Gap: Why Integrating High School with College Makes Sense and How to Do It.* Cambridge, Mass.: Harvard Education Press, 2007.

North Carolina General Assembly. *Report to the Joint Legislative Education Oversight Committee: Learn and Earn Early College High School Initiative.* 2008.

NANCY HOFFMAN *is vice president of Youth Transitions and director of the Early College High School Initiative at Jobs for the Future, a nonprofit research, consulting, and advocacy organization.*

JOEL VARGAS *works with the Early College High School Initiative at Jobs for the Future, examining related district and state policy implications.*

JANET SANTOS *is a project manager at Jobs for the Future, where she develops and advocates policies to increase students' academic achievement and high school completion rates.*

3

*Although the transition from high school to college is a
predictable rite of passage for students in their late teens
and early twenties, much about the nature of these
students and their environments is changing.*

New Challenges in Working with Traditional-Aged College Students

Jennifer R. Keup

Each year, millions of new students enter colleges and universities across
the country. Although many of these students are older than the traditional
age of college entry, the vision of a "college student" as represented in literature, legend, cartoon, film, television, and even scholarly research is still
that of the young student fresh from high school. In fact, a significant majority of first-year students are traditional aged (Pryor, Hurtado, Sharkness, and
Korn, 2007). These students seventeen to twenty years old who have
matriculated to college directly from high school with little or no break in
their educational experience (inclusive of winter admits and students engaging in a gap year experience) are the focus of this chapter.

Somewhat paradoxically, recent literature has indicated that the current
crop of traditional first-year students is qualitatively different from their predecessors. Generational theorists, most notably Strauss and Howe (1991,
2006), have identified individuals born between 1982 and 2002, today's traditional college students, as a new generation with a significantly different
"peer personality" from its predecessors, a group that has earned the
moniker *millennials*. According to Howe and Strauss (2000), millennials
are optimistic, high achieving, civic minded, and moral, and they hold the
promise of true greatness. Their potential lies in their extreme intelligence,
enthusiastic involvement, group orientation, respect for authority, extraor-
dinary drive, greater comfort with technology, and an increased experience
with diversity with respect to both personal identity and in society at large
(Brooks, 2001; Keeling, 2003; Newton, 2000; Pryor, Hurtado, Saenz, and
others, 2007). However, along with these good qualities also come others,

NEW DIRECTIONS FOR HIGHER EDUCATION, no. 144, Winter 2008 © Wiley Periodicals, Inc.
Published online in Wiley InterScience (www.interscience.wiley.com) • DOI: 10.1002/he.323

including a capacity to follow rather than to lead, an absence of true intellectual curiosity, excessive collectivism, a lack of true self-awareness, and relatively few sociopolitical passions (Brooks, 2001; Howe and Strauss, 2000; Keeling, 2003; Newton, 2000).

These generational characteristics and forces have led to a rethinking of perennial concerns in higher education such as effective pedagogy, student engagement, and personal development. However, other new issues that have an effect on the transition experience of today's traditional-aged students are also gaining the attention of campus-based practitioners as well as the national media. Among these many issues, I focus on four that I believe are of particular significance: (1) the shift to a truly multicultural student body, (2) burgeoning mental and emotional health care needs, (3) students' overwhelmingly vocational or utilitarian view of higher education, and (4) the integration of new technologies in the life of college students. Higher educational professionals, especially those who work with first-year students, have made these four issues the focus of recent research and writing (Koch and others, 2007). (Chapter Four in this volume addresses another important issue of contemporary campus life: parental involvement in the lives of today's college students.)

Multiculturalism

Even when constrained by a focus on only traditional students, the dawn of the new millennium has seen a more diverse traditional first-year student population than ever before. Today this population includes greater representation of various cultures, religions, races/ethnicities, native languages, degrees of physical ability, sexual orientation, levels of academic preparation, socioeconomic backgrounds, family structure, and high school experiences and preparation (Crissman Ishler, 2005; National Center for Education Statistics, 2005; Pryor and others, 2007; Pryor, Hurtado, Sharkness, and Korn, 2007; Upcraft, Gardner, and Barefoot, 2005; U.S. Census Bureau, 2005). Underrepresented racial and ethnic groups have made significant inroads with respect to college enrollment and persistence, such that they now represent more than 25 percent of the traditional college-going population (National Center for Education Statistics, 2005).

Although most of these statistics are encouraging with respect to larger goals related to access and success for all first-year students, they do not fully explain the issue of how diversity affects the transition of traditional first-year students, whether they are members of a majority or minority group. A growing issue within the diversity dialogue is that many colleges and universities today enroll students who are part of different groups within and between categories of personal identity and background. These students interpret their own personal identity and gauge the diversity of their environments from a pluralistic viewpoint (Jones and McEwen, 2000). For instance, on the 2000 U.S. Census, 4 percent of the population under age eighteen was identified as multiracial (Greico and Casssidy, 2001). Population projections indicate that multiracial individuals will make up 21 percent of the population at large by the year 2050 (Root, 1999; Harper, 2007). Although representation from diverse and multicultural backgrounds varies widely by region of the country, areas where there is the greatest diversity are truly the bellwether rather than the anomaly.

Higher education is attempting to capture these demographic changes among traditional students in assessment and reporting systems—most notably as students enter college and are identified in admissions and registration—as well as in the institution's intervention strategies. However, students are constantly outpacing our capacity to categorize them. Colleges have never been less equipped with an effective vocabulary and schema to discuss diversity, and many higher education professionals are uncomfortable with the ambiguity that accompanies this topic. As such, millennial students who are in the earlier stages of personal development may not feel encouraged to examine all areas of their own identity or feel comfortable with their peers who integrate multiple aspects (race/ethnicity, religion, sexual orientation, and so forth) into their core identity. Conversely, traditional-aged students who enter college with a core sense of self that integrates multiple identities may not feel they fit in the mutually exclusive categories typically used to track diversity in higher education. Furthermore, the transition experience of these students may be one in which they do not feel recognized, safe, and supported as they continue to hold on to and explore various elements of their core identity during their transition to the college or university.

Given that the overall trend of diversification is expected to persist, campus personnel must continue to work toward shaping a truly multicultural college environment that facilitates diversity experiences for all students. This is a particularly important goal for first-year-experience programs since the first year is the point of students' initial interactions with institutional culture. This period also sets the precedent for students' interaction and comfort in the campus climate.

First-year-experience educators need to identify how their programs, policies, and pedagogies capitalize on the multiple perspectives traditional college students bring with them—perspectives that contribute to the total campus environment. To facilitate a successful transition for all students, educators should acknowledge elements of the historical and campus context related to the diversity and should understand the impact of institutional messages being conveyed about the value of diversity as it relates to new students' personal identity and interpersonal interactions.

Mental and Emotional Health

As a result of tragic acts of violence on several college campuses, the nation has been made aware of the mental and emotional health care needs among traditional-aged college students. These events have brought widespread attention to this issue, but higher education professionals have long been aware of this growing problem and have all but identified it as a hallmark of the millennial generation.

National data indicate that current cohorts of students are facing significant issues related to their overall health and well-being. However, while college students' self-ratings of physical health decline during the first year of college and approximately one-quarter express some concern about their health, statistics related to students' emotional health are far more troubling. In particular, self-ratings of emotional health among traditional first-year students experienced significant declines in the 1990s and have hovered at their lowest rates since 2000 (Pryor, Hurtado, Saenz, and others, 2007). These same national statistics reveal slight increases in depression among students during the first year and significant growth in the proportion of students who feel overwhelmed. In addition, students are engaging in fewer stress-reducing and leisure activities such as exercising and sports and reading for pleasure, and they are drinking and partying more often during the first year of college than they did in high school. Furthermore, current cohorts of traditional college students are relying more heavily on their parents for emotional support than their predecessors did (College Parents of America, 2007; Keup and Stolzenberg, 2004; Pryor, Hurtado, Sharkness, and Korn, 2007).

These increases in rates of depression and anxiety, coupled with decreases in self-ratings of emotional and physical health, are a concern in and of themselves. However, these statistics are only symptoms of a much larger issue: greater numbers of traditional college students are dealing with significant, and often more severe, psychological problems and emotional health issues than in previous decades (Crissman Ishler, 2005; Kitzrow, 2003; Levine and Cureton, 1998). While some of these issues emerge during the college years, more students are entering higher education with at least moderate, if not severe, symptoms of psychological distress. More specifically, findings from the 2004 National Survey of Counseling Center Directors at 334 colleges across the country are that during the 2003–2004 year, 2,200 students were hospitalized for psychological reasons and 137 students committed suicide. In addition, there were rising numbers of student self-injury cases and significant increases in the proportion of students who were already on psychotropic medications (Gallagher, 2004). Directors also reported that over 40 percent of their clients have "severe psychological problems [and] 8.7% have impairments so serious that they cannot remain in school or can only do so with extensive psychological/-psychiatric help" (p. 2).

A certain level of stress and emotional discomfort can be expected for new college students and is even perhaps necessary for a meaningful transition. Test anxiety, arguments with roommates, homesickness, and romantic heartbreaks represent predictable rites of passage for first-year college students. Yet because traditional students have grown up in a youth culture in which they have been shielded from failure, have developed less resiliency, and are less experienced dealing with conflict without parental intervention, the tipping point where regular stress turns into an emotional crisis is much lower than for previous generations. As such, it often seems as if the young men and women entering colleges and universities today are only a few bad days away from significant depression, debilitating anxiety, or substance misuse and abuse. Since emotional and mental health problems are associated with lower levels of social integration, academic performance, and persistence to the second year (Kitzrow, 2003; Perrine, 2001; Pritchard and Wilson, 2003), students' mental and emotional health needs are of great concern to first-year-experience professionals.

As with many other challenges in higher education, recognizing this issue and finding the resources to deal with it effectively are very different matters. Data show that fiscal and human resources dedicated to campus counseling centers have not experienced increases commensurate with growing need among millennial students (Gallagher, 2004; Kitzrow, 2003). As such, student psychological services are often taxed beyond capacity. This leaves a significant number of students who are dealing with more predictable emotional crises with only the help they can find from concerned faculty, staff, and peers who, however well intentioned, are often unprepared to address emotional and mental health care needs.

Since points of transition represent a time when individuals are more prone to psychological distress, first-year programs and personnel are in a position to lead institutional and national efforts to address this issue effectively. Preterm orientation, extended orientation-style first-year seminars, and residential life programs for new students have incorporated programs that familiarize students with campus physical and emotional health services. But relegating information about these services to a single program or class session is not enough. Entire campus communities must become more aware of students who exhibit warning signs and symptoms of emotional distress and must provide essential resources to support their psychological health and well-being.

Redefining the Purpose of College

Why do students attend college? Of the several possible answers to that question, many of today's first-year students are likely to respond "to get a job" or, more specifically, "to get a good job." Educators often assume that community or technical college students are more likely to focus their education on job preparation than are students at baccalaureate campuses. But this same vocational perspective is voiced by many first-year students, whether they begin college in the two-year or four-year sector. New students are often intolerant of courses or activities not directly related to their intended major or career path, and they complain bitterly about what they refer to as "irrelevant" general education courses such as history, foreign language, or even English composition. This disinterest in broad liberal learning results in disengagement in many first-year classes and diminishes the quality of the academic transition through the first, and perhaps even the second, year of college.

Over forty years ago, Burton Clark and Martin Trow (1966) identified four dominant student subcultures in higher education, which remain particularly useful descriptors for traditional college students (Feldman and Newcomb, 1969). These subcultures emerge from the combination of two variables: students' involvement with ideas (much or little) and students' identification with their college (much or little). The *academic subculture* represents students who are invested in their college and in ideas; *nonconformists* share the academics' interest in ideas but not their identification with the institution. Students in the *collegiate subculture* are very engaged in the institution, but are typically involved outside the realm of academics, and students in the *vocational subculture* are not invested in the intellectual ideas of the institution and do not identify with the institution.

While this typology of student subcultures was developed at an earlier time of generational shift, it is still useful for today's traditional student subcultures. Today many traditional-aged entering students can be characterized as belonging to the vocational subculture. They are no longer "intellectual blank slates that are ripe with intellectual curiosity and hungering for their consciousness to be awakened" (Lang, 2008, p. C1).

National data sources on traditional-aged first-year college students indicate significant shifts in students' core values over the past several decades that help explain this phenomenon. In the late 1960s, "developing a meaningful philosophy of life" was reported as being very important or essential by the majority of entering students (86 percent). Only 42 percent indicated that "being very well off financially" was a core value (Pryor, Hurtado, Saenz, and others, 2007). In the 1980s and 1990s, these benchmark core values essentially switched places, and financial interests have remained a greater personal priority for the majority of traditional college students ever since.

In 2006, just over 75 percent of entering traditional college students reported that the desire to "learn about things that interest me" was a very important reason in deciding to go to college, but approximately 70 percent of the same students indicated that the ability to make more money, get a better job, and gain training in a specific career were similarly important motivators for their pursuit of a degree (Pryor, Hurtado, Saenz, and others, 2007).

The fact that traditional first-year students appear to be entering college for the primary purpose of career training, professional or graduate school preparation, and financial security should come as no surprise given the extremely high costs to attend college and the significant educational debt many students face at graduation. And to some, this push and pull between liberal education and the more utilitarian vocational interests of students may represent opposite ideals. However, our challenge with respect to serving today's traditional students is to blend these two worlds and make the exposure and skill development that is gained from a liberal arts education relevant to students' interests and aspirations. Carol Geary Schneider (2006), president of the Association of American Colleges and Universities, wrote about this challenge:

> Today's college students should not be presented with a false choice between either vocational preparation or liberal-arts education defined as nonvocational personal development. It is time to embrace a far more purposeful approach to college that sets clear expectations for all students, cultivates the achievement of a set of essential skills and capacities, and enables every student to place his or her interests—including career aspirations—in the broader context of a complex and fast-changing world [p. B17].

Technology

In the not-too-distant past, discussions of technology in the college environment were primarily limited to computer access. It has actually been during the lifetime of millennials that a personal computer became virtually universal for students at colleges and universities. In 1985, fewer than 30 percent of students reported frequent use of personal computers; by 1995, this percentage was over 50 percent (Pryor, Hurtado, Saenz, and others, 2007). Recent statistics show that 86 percent of first-time, first-year students at four-year universities reported using a computer frequently, and nearly all reported using it at least occasionally (Pryor, Hurtado, Saenz, and others 2007). Furthermore, at least 85 percent of college students own a computer (Junco, 2005). Although there are still inequities with respect to technology access and utilization among minority racial/ethnic groups, as well as students from rural areas and lower socioeconomic backgrounds, today's traditional college students overall have been exposed to a wide array of personal computing options and technologies and enjoy easy access to them.

During these past few decades, higher education has incorporated technology into the learning process. For example, faculty communicate and counsel by e-mail, online enrollment is becoming the norm, library materials are being moved to online formats, electronic academic portfolios are gaining in popularity, and nearly 80 percent of traditional first-year students report that they use the Internet for research or homework (Pryor, Hurtado, Saenz, and others, 2007). While faculty and administrators at higher education institutions often express concerns that technology is replacing face-to-face faculty-student contact to the detriment of learning, students perceive that these technologies, particularly those related to the Internet, are academically beneficial. Just under half report that e-mail allows them to express ideas to a professor that they would not express in person, approximately two-thirds subscribe to a listserv related to their academic discipline, and 79 percent report that the Internet has had a positive impact on their academics (Pew Internet and American Life Project, 2000). These perceived

New Directions for Higher Education • DOI: 10.1002/he

outcomes on the part of the student are triangulated by recent data from the National Survey of Student Engagement (2007) that when "used appropriately, technology facilitates learning and promotes collaboration among peers and instructors" (p. 47).

A more recent trend among millennials is their use of computer and telecommunication technologies in the social realm. The more widespread use of e-mail and the birth of social networking sites and instant messaging capabilities have changed the way that today's students meet and socialize with their institutional peers, maintain contact and connections with family, and stay in touch with high school friends in other locations. More and more students maintain multiple e-mail accounts, social networking sites, and phone numbers, and they use instant messaging and text messaging daily. These advancements in communication technology have been cited as one of the primary reasons for college students' continuing reliance on their parents during the first-year transition and the emergence of "helicopter parents" (Henning, 2007).

The ease with which students communicate and share information is changing their process of integration during the transition from high school to college, their connection to the campus community, and expectations regarding interpersonal communication. Information technologies are a significant contributor to the consumer mentality of today's college students (Levine and Cureton, 1998). Anecdotes exchanged around staff and faculty coffee klatches on campus often include complaints of students who were irritated because their 3:00 A.M. e-mail to a professor was not answered by the start of morning class that same day, misuse of professors' home and cell phone numbers so that students can get an immediate answer to their questions, or students' fielding cell phone calls, e-mails, and text messages during class.

Residential life staff can contribute their own stories about how information technologies have changed the nature of students' interactions with roommates, neighbors, and staff as students choose virtual means of communication and conflict resolution over face-to-face interactions. Who has not heard the anecdote about the two roommates who sat back to back in silence while they argued using instant messaging, or the story about students who were outraged at being disciplined for violating campus policy regarding the posting of offensive pictures on the public portion of their social networking sites?

While at times these examples may be humorous, they also illustrate significant challenges of managing students' expectations about interaction with one another and the college or university. In its most benign form, more social uses of technology represent a challenge to students' time management, and in a more serious light, they represent the potential breakdown of interpersonal skill development, conflict resolution, and management of one's personal information and safety. The challenge is that the development of interpersonal communication skills and personal management, which may be lost due to technological advances, rivals, if not surpasses, knowledge about the many applications of technology as critical to future personal, professional, and educational success.

Conclusion

When this generation of students has left the college or university for life beyond and when those of us who serve them are facing retirement, these four issues—multiculturalism, mental and emotional health care, students' narrow perceptions about the purpose of higher education, and technology—will be remembered as some of the greatest challenges confronting both students and educators in the early years of the twenty-first century. Yet these issues also give rise to significant contributions of knowledge and best practice for future generations of educators.

In dealing with these challenges, it is important to remember that students and their development are at the foundation of our work. It may be tempting to think about these issues first from the perspective of their impact on institutions rather than their impact on students. For example, students' mental health care needs often lead to concerns about institutional liability, and conversations about technology often focus on campus capacity and service delivery. Similarly, conversations about student diversity initiatives may drift into a discussion of admission policies and retention rates, and expanding on students' vocational perception of college is relegated to a career center or considered a failing of general education. In all of our attempts to work with traditional students, first-year-experience professionals have the opportunity to focus or refocus conversations, campus policies, and resource allocation on the essential task of easing students' educational and developmental transitions.

References

Brooks, D. "The Organization Kid." *Atlantic Monthly,* Apr. 2001, pp. 40–54.

College Parents of America. "Second Annual National Survey on College Parent Experiences: Executive Summary and Analysis." 2007. Retrieved Nov. 1, 2007, from http://www.collegeparents.org/files/2007-Current-Parent-Survey-Summary.pdf.

Clark, B., and Trow, M. "The Organizational Context. " In T. Newcomb and E. Wilson (eds.), *College Peer Groups: Problems and Prospects for Research.* Chicago: Aldine, 1966.

Crissman Ishler, J. L. "Today's First-Year Students." In M. L. Upcraft and others (eds.), *Challenging and Supporting the First-Year Student: A Handbook for Improving the First Year of College.* San Francisco: Jossey-Bass, 2005.

Feldman, K. A., and Newcomb, T. M. *The Impact of College on Students.* San Francisco: Jossey-Bass, 1969.

Gallagher, R. P. *National Survey of Counseling Center Directors.* Pittsburgh, Pa.: International Association of Counseling Services, 2004.

Greico, E. M., and Cassidy, R. C. *Overview of Race and Hispanic Origin: Census 2000 Brief.* Washington, D.C.: U.S. Department of Commerce, Economics and Statistics Administration, 2001. Retrieved Apr. 28, 2006, from www.census.gov/population/www/cen2000/briefs.html.

Harper, C. E. "Count Me In: A Mixed-Methods Analysis of the Theoretical, Methodological, and Practical Implications of Accounting for Multiracial Backgrounds in Higher Education," Unpublished doctoral dissertation, University of California, Los Angeles, 2007.

Henning, G. "Is *In Consortio Cum Parentibus* the New *In Loco Parentis?*" *NASPA Journal,* 2007, *44,* 538–559.

Howe, N., and Strauss, W. *Millennials Rising: The Next Great Generation.* New York: Vintage Books, 2000.

Jones, S. R., and McEwen, M. K. "A Conceptual Model of Multiple Dimensions of Identity." *Journal of College Student Development,* 2000, *41,* 405–414.

Junco, R. "Technology and Today's First-Year College Student." In M. L. Upcraft and others (eds.), *Challenging and Supporting the First-Year Student: A Handbook for Improving the First Year of College.* San Francisco: Jossey-Bass, 2005.

Keeling, S. "Advising the Millennial Generation." *Journal of the National Academic Advising Association,* 2003, *23,* 30–36.

Keup, J. R., and Stolzenberg, E. B. *The 2003 Your First College Year (YCY) Survey: Exploring the Academic and Personal Experiences of First-Year Students.* Columbia: University of South Carolina, National Resource Center for The First-Year Experience and Students in Transition, 2007.

Kitzrow, M. A. "The Mental Health Care Needs of Today's College Students: Challenges and Recommendations." *NASPA Journal,* 2003, *41,* 167–181.

Koch, A. K., and others. (eds.). *The First-Year Experience in American Higher Education: An Annotated Bibliography.* (4th ed.) Columbia: University of South Carolina, National Resource Center for The First-Year Experience and Students in Transition, 2007.

Lang, J. A. "The Myth of First-Year Enlightenment." *Chronicle of Higher Education,* Feb. 1, 2008. Retrieved May 12, 2008, from http://chronicle.com/jobs/news/2008/02/2008020101c/.html.

Levine, A., and Cureton, J. A. *When Hope and Fear Collide.* San Francisco: Jossey-Bass, 1998.

National Center for Educational Statistics. *The Condition of Education, 2005.* Washington, DC: U.S. Government Printing Office, 2005.

National Survey of Student Engagement. *Experiences That Matter: Enhancing Student Learning and Success, Annual Report 2007.* Bloomington: Center for Postsecondary Research, Indiana University, 2007.

Newton, F. B. "The New Student," *About Campus,* 2000, *5*(5), 8–15.

Perrine, R. M. "College Stress and Persistence as a Function of Attachment and Support." *Journal of The First-Year Experience and Students in Transition,* 2001, *13*(1), 7–22.

Pew Internet and American Life Project. *Tracking Online Life: How Women Use the Internet to Cultivate Relationships with Family and Friends,* May 10, 2000. Retrieved Feb. 6, 2008, from http://www.pewinternet.org/pdfs/Report1.pdf.

Pritchard, M. E., and Wilson, G. S. "Using Emotional and Social Factors to Predict Student Success." *Journal of College Student Development,* 2003, *44,* 18–28.

Pryor, J. H., Hurtado, S., Sharkness, J., and Korn, W. S. *The American Freshman: National Norms For Fall 2007.* Los Angeles: University of California Los Angeles, Higher Education Research Institute, 2007.

Pryor, J. H., Hurtado, S., Saenz, V. B., and others. *The American Freshman: Forty Year Trends.* Los Angeles: University of California Los Angeles, Higher Education Research Institute, 2007.

Root, M. P. "The Biracial Baby Boom: Understanding Ecological Constructions of Racial Identity in the 21st Century." In R. H. Sheets and E. R. Hollins (eds.), *Racial and Ethnic Identity in School Practices: Aspects of Human Development.* Mahwah, N.J.: Erlbaum, 1999.

Schneider, C. G. "Educating Students to Earn a Living, and to Live." *Chronicle of Higher Education,* Aug. 4, 2006. Retrieved May 18, 2008, from http://chronicle.com/weekly/v52/i48/48b01701.htm.

Strauss, W., and Howe, N. *Generations: The History of America's Future, 1584–2069.* New York: HarperCollins, 1991.

Strauss, W., and Howe, N. *Millennials and the Pop Culture: Strategies for a New Generation of Consumers in Music, Movies, Television, the Internet, and Video Games.* Great Falls, Va.: LifeCourse Associates, 2006.

Upcraft, M. L., Gardner, J. N., and Barefoot, B. O. (eds). *Challenging and Supporting the First-Year College Student.* San Francisco: Jossey-Bass, 2005.

U.S. Census Bureau. *School Enrollment: Social and Economic Characteristics of Students: October, 2003.* Washington, D.C.: U.S. Department of Commerce, 2003.

JENNIFER R. KEUP is director of the National Resource Center for The First Year Experience and Students in Transition at the University of South Carolina.

Parents of college students influence the transition experiences of their sons and daughters, and they also experience significant transitions of their own.

From Helicopter Parent to Valued Partner: Shaping the Parental Relationship for Student Success

Marc Cutright

I start with a confession: I have been one. A helicopter parent, so named for hovering over a college student—my college student, my daughter—when the college professionals thought it would be better to leave her problems to them.

Now the defense. My daughter asked me to intervene with her college when a squirrel was scampering, day and night, in the wall of her room. No, I said, and I gave her some tips on how to get it taken care of. The college came right out and sealed the hole in the exterior wall—with an increasingly frantic squirrel trapped inside. THEN I started making calls, knowing that an "embrace the bureaucracy" lesson could be pursued another day. Did I do the right thing? Can't say.

But plenty of professionals in student affairs would say no. They decry the involvement of parents, which is happening at levels of intensity and in matters of minutiae they say they have never before witnessed. They tell "can-you-top-this" stories in person and in print about moms who call the college president seeking redress of an unfairly given grade of B, and dads who rail red-faced about never giving the institution another dime if the dean does not report to him on Junior's suspected nightlife and resulting absence from 8:00 A.M. biology classes (Strauss, 2006; Colavecchio-Van Sickler, 2006).

But I know another story, told to me by a colleague who works at a small community college in the Blue Ridge Mountains of Virginia. Many people there

NEW DIRECTIONS FOR HIGHER EDUCATION, no. 144, Winter 2008 © Wiley Periodicals, Inc.
Published online in Wiley InterScience (www.interscience.wiley.com) • DOI: 10.1002/he.324

are poor and not formally schooled past very basic levels. My friend had witnessed a new student, a young woman, who came to school one day with younger siblings, parents, and grandparents in tow. They wanted to witness and celebrate a momentous family occasion: the young lady registering for classes for the first time, the first such toe in college waters by any member of the family ever. There were smiles and tears over an event that the more jaded among us consider just another bureaucratic hassle of institutional life.

Where is the truth of parental involvement and concern in these extremes? Is parental involvement a problem to be monitored like a communicable disease, something about which we can share funny stories and strategies for containment? Or is it the manifestation of deep emotions—love, hope, fear—that we have both an opportunity and an obligation to address? The short answer is yes.

The fact is that parents are not a monolithic crowd. They are neither overbearing second-guessers who will not let their children grow and mature, nor a purely benevolent but naive set of bystanders, waiting to be called on before they make any interventions and leaving it to the professionals. Parents are rational and emotional, informed and misinformed, deeply interested and distressingly distant, seeking solutions to and being part of various problems.

We can say, however, that the environment in which students and parents find themselves as they enter college in the early twenty-first century is very different than it was even a few years ago. These are some elements of those differences.

The law regulating the complex relationships of parents, students, and institutions is shifting, murky, and challenging.

The ideal for many parents of in loco parentis—the college acting in place of parents in the monitoring and regulation of student behavior in and out of the classroom—is dead. It has been weakened by various statutes and legal decisions going back more than a century, but the independence of students from institutional control has accelerated in recent decades (Bickel and Lake, 1999).

The foment of campus politics during the 1960s empowered student independence and assertion of rights. The constitutional amendment giving eighteen year olds the right to vote led a shift in the general legal environment toward regarding the age of eighteen, rather than twenty-one, as the threshold of legal majority. The federal Buckley Amendment, later evolving into today's Family Educational Rights and Privacy Act (FERPA), prohibited the sharing of individual student information with virtually anyone, including the student's parents. While modifications have been included to allow institutional communication with parents in the cases of a student's physical and mental well-being and for some circumstances of drug and alcohol use, FERPA still prohibits in large the ability of colleges to communicate with parents about attendance,

NEW DIRECTIONS FOR HIGHER EDUCATION • DOI: 10.1002/he

grades, or other matters once clearly within the domain of in loco parentis (Bowden, 2007; Henning, 2007; Bickel and Lake, 1999).

The shifts in legal environment have occurred when, ironically, campuses have been held accountable to new laws and regulations about the environments they provide for students. The Cleary Act of 1990, named for a campus murder victim, held campuses responsible by federal law for the uniform compilation, and reporting to both the government and the public, of campus crime statistics. Legal actions and suits, sometimes successful, have been leveled against institutions for an asserted failure to act and share information in a timely fashion about students who exhibit self-destructive behaviors. Of increasing concern to campus officials, students, and parents is the presence on college campuses of students with diagnosed mental problems that could lead (and have led) to highly violent behavior toward others. In retrospect, which is how case law is made, decisions and their wisdom are sometimes clearer. In real time, the conflicting assertions of student privacy, parental interests, and even such laws as the Health Insurance Portability and Accountability Act, which is steadfast in the protection of patient privacy, put all parties in positions that can seem no-win and legally perilous regardless of action.

It is no wonder, then, that parents assert rights that they may or may not have when laws are conflicting and basic circumstances so different from those of the parents' college days. Even seasoned campus officials often have to talk to the campus lawyer before acting in complex circumstances.

Communications are ubiquitous and continuous.

The 1970s and 1980s, when many of today's parents were in college, were times when communications with parents in a distant city were restricted to visits home, actual put-a-stamp-on-it mail, and maybe a weekly call on the residence hall's pay phone. Today most colleges have quickly made the transition from putting phones in every residence hall room to removing them, since "everyone" has a cell phone or prefers to communicate by e-mail, instant messaging, or text messaging.

A class exercise for my graduate students who are preparing for careers in student affairs professions is a schedule of structured interviews with first-year students about their lifestyles and time management. Some questions relate to communications with parents. Five phone calls home a day to parents or siblings in a distant city is on the higher end of staying-in-touch patterns but not particularly unusual. Some students do not own alarm clocks or use their cell phones as substitute alarms, but instead get the same daily rousing by telephone from their parents that they got back in high school. Dad and Mom still help with homework, but while daughter or son is walking with friends to the coffee shop.

Are these circumstances of a failure to let go and grow up, or a tool of keeping families connected in supportive ways that contribute to student success? As with most other complex circumstances, it depends.

Expectations of the college-going environment are affected by consumerism.

Rankings from *U.S. News & World Report, Money Magazine,* and a dozen other sources encourage us to look at college education as a commodity that can be compared by using about the same number of metrics one might use to decide among new cars. Tuition rates that have risen more steadily than general inflation for decade after decade, no matter the justifications, have resulted in price tags that can make a college education the most costly expenditure of a lifetime. The cumulative national debt from student loans, as the country has moved from governmental grants to individual responsibility for college finance, combined with bankruptcy laws that now make it virtually impossible to discharge the burdens due to hardship, have led some to speculate that even more serious economic troubles are on the way.

When students and parents cannot count on much help to pay for college and when the sticker price is indeed shocking, it is little wonder that values shift from college education as a societal good to college education as a personal investment and possession. With that values system comes assertion of "property" rights: expectations of services on demands, even if not offered by the college; rights to know how money is used, both generally and on behalf of an individual; and a general assumption by some parents that the customer is always right.

Parents come to college with a gamut of personal knowledge about college and how it works.

A premier condition of American higher education has been the trend since World War II of democratization and massification, that is, a general interest in seeing both that everyone has a chance to go to college and that society benefits from high levels of advanced education. With postsecondary participation rates by eighteen- to twenty-four-year-olds of nearly 50 percent, and more among some demographic sectors, the Untied States enjoys one of the world's highest rates of inclusion (National Center for Education Statistics, 2005).

Yet it is sometimes easy to forget that if half of our potential students are in attendance, half are not. If we do our jobs well and continue to make advances in rates of participation, particularly among historically underrepresented populations, we will see lots of first-generation college students for a long time to come.

Parents come to colleges and universities with variable levels of college understanding. Some hold graduate degrees, have attended four or five institutions, have put several children through college before, and can easily and comfortably speak to a professor. For others, this is uncharted territory, and even the jargon is opaque. I recall a friend who was just short of a college degree discussing the circumstances with her father who had never himself attended. "How much more do you have to do?" he asked. "Three hours," she replied. "Three hours? Aren't you off work on Friday? Just go over and take care of it." And in a world where a three-hour responsibility can be discharged before lunch, that is a completely reasonable suggestion.

The challenge for educators is providing information that assists, comforts, educates, and enlists parents as educational partners, but does all of this across the range of knowledge and background that parents present. Efforts aimed exclusively at one or the other end of this range will, by definition, leave out about half of all parents.

Love is all around us.
The most rewarding, vexing, or infuriating of parental interactions with colleges tend to share a common factor: heavy emotional context, be it anger, fear, or joy. And these originate in the reality of parent and child love, something we can too easily forget. If parents sometimes seem irrational, it might be worth asking if our own closest relationships always run smoothly and logically. Often situations are best handled or substantially improved simply by lowering the temperature of the emotional environment, expressing real empathy, and explicitly committing to work through the issue.

What Colleges Can Do

Colleges and universities can take a number of intentional steps to work more collaboratively with parents. These actions will increase parental understanding of the collegiate environment and build connections that support student success.

The Partnership Relationship. An underlying philosophy that strengthens most institutional-parental contexts is the deliberate effort to establish a partnership relationship with parents. This offsets the adversarial relationship that can emerge in the absence of an effort to shape interactions.

Many institutions find the idea of familial relationships to be an even stronger and more cohesive conceptual framework. Family relationships involve deep emotional connections, rights to speak and be considered in decisions, an evolving maturity and focus based on time, and commitments to stick with one another through thick and thin. For most institutions, that kind of relationship with parents, although fairly "high maintenance," is more productive than the contractual, consumerist one that it displaces.

Orientation as an Event and as a Process. Many institutions now have orientation sessions for parents that parallel the orientation sessions they hold for students (Mullendore and Banahan, 2005). These are typically one-day, sometimes two-day, events on campus, often held while students themselves are participating in conventional orientation activities. Content frequently includes extensive information about what students will be doing in coming days and weeks, expectations of students, a review of relevant law (particularly FERPA), the college social environment and how students will be encouraged to handle and balance it, the changes in students that parents are likely to witness, and how parents can support students' successful transition.

New Directions for Higher Education • DOI: 10.1002/he

It is important that educators seize such opportunities to pull parents into the partnership that supports student success. Partnership involves not only rights but responsibilities. Educators should be forthright not only about the behaviors and approaches that contribute to students' accepting responsibility, but also about behaviors that inhibit independence and the acceptance of personal responsibility. Discussions that involve parents and upper-level student leaders are one mechanism to deal with specific issues. By avoiding direct reference to the potential problems that can be caused by "incoming" parents, situations can be worked through hypothetically and will be easier to deal with when encountered in real life.

It is also helpful to look at orientation not just as a one-time event but as a continuing process (Mullendore and Banahan, 2005). The need for and interest in information and institutional interaction begins long before formal orientation on campus, and many issues that an orientation session might cover will not be relevant until months into the future. Orientation for parents therefore should ideally begin with the first evidence of interest in the institution and continue well into the first year of college. Some functions that go beyond college orientation, such as the cultivation and solicitation of parents as financial contributors, will go on well beyond orientation. Internet-based communications and e-mail present major low-cost opportunities for just-in-time delivery of key information to parents, but sole dependence on Internet communication will mean that parents without computer access or computer literacy will miss important information.

Handbooks and Similar Print Materials. Just as colleges use handbooks for students, often combined with an appointment and event calendar, so they can use handbooks for parents. The handbook represents not only another communication mechanism, one that virtually everyone can use; it also offers parents an opportunity to take in key information when they have a particular need to know. Very detailed information can be communicated through a handbook in ways that Internet-based or in-person communications do less effectively.

The use of print communications with parents, particularly those that are mailed or otherwise distributed outside a formal, more content-controlled environment such as orientation sessions, raises the possibility of communication overload or overlap from multiple offices. It is even possible that various well-meaning administrators can give conflicting advice and information. It is worthwhile for a person or office with top responsibility for parent communications to act as a clearinghouse for all messages intended for parents. Even the function of smoothing the information delivery schedule, so that five mailings are not received on one day and none for another month, is a service to the institution and parents and increases the chance that each message will be regarded more closely.

Whom to Contact. One of the elements frequently heard in stories about helicopter parents is the petitioning of inappropriate officials at the university about student issues, such as calling the president about a lack of hot water in a residence hall, visiting the provost about a poor grade, and requesting the dean to monitor a student's getting out of bed and to class on time. Some of that comes from a misplaced concept of getting things done by "going straight to the top," but some of it comes from a lack of information about appropriate channels to bring up issues, regardless of their ultimate importance or appropriateness.

It is preferable for colleges to anticipate parental concerns and to offer clear, readily available recommendations about the individuals whom parents might contact to seek assistance with different problems or questions. Names, telephone numbers, and e-mail addresses are important; giving only general office contacts is impersonal and increases the chances that such offers of assistance will be bypassed to "go to the top."

Knowing What FERPA Prohibits, and What It Does Not. FERPA, in theory, is a sound articulation of student independence and adulthood. In practice, it has sometimes inhibited institutional-parental consultation when that consultation is appropriate to the student's best interests. But the fact is that colleges have tended to be inhibited in their parental communications by believing that FERPA and subsequent modifications prohibit communications that it in fact does not prohibit, according to LeRoy Rooker (2008), an attorney with the U.S. Department of Education.

FERPA gives students the right to inspect and review all educational records including, but not limited to, grade records and to seek amendments to those records. FERPA also gives students some, but not unlimited, control over the disclosure of those records to others. Exceptions to FERPA include records created and maintained by law enforcement agencies; those records are not protected from disclosure beyond the rights extended to any citizen. The Health Insurance Portability and Accountability Act is generally very restrictive of disclosure. But FERPA specifically trumps it when a record may fall under both considerations.

Other exceptions to the prohibition on disclosure of a student's records to parents under FERPA include the following:

- Results of a disciplinary hearing if a student is in violation and the violation involves violence
- Violations of drug or alcohol policies if the student is under twenty-one years old
- Disclosure of relevant information that is deemed necessary to protect the health or safety of the student or others
- Disclosure of educational records when the student is a tax dependent

Additional liberalizations of the ability to disclose information were under consideration by the federal government at the time of this writing. For most current and detailed information, consult the Web site of the U.S. Department of Education's Family Policy Compliance Office (http://www.ed.gov/policy/gen/guid/fpco/index.html).

FERPA rights may be waived by a student who gives informed consent and a signature. Standardized forms are available for waiver of confidentiality. It might be appropriate to use such waivers, for example, as a condition of participation in a special academic recovery or readmission program, as some institutions have done. Such actions create an opportunity to communicate with parents and are part of an intensive, ongoing advising and monitoring program intended to get the student back into good academic standing. The permission to waive FERPA rights would likely expire when the student had regained full academic status. Waivers, however, are themselves subject to particular limitations. They must specify the records that may be disclosed and state the reason for the disclosure. Furthermore, they must identify, by name or status ("my parents"), the individuals to whom disclosure can be made.

Resources for Parents, Students, and Educators

College Parents of America is a national membership organization dedicated to informing parents about key general issues of college attendance and public and legislative advocacy on behalf of those families. A number of colleges and universities are institutional members of the organization.

Several college-related professional organizations are also involved in improving parent-institution relationships. The National Association of Student Personnel Administrators (NASPA) sponsors a "knowledge community" to consider parent and family relations. A section of the organization's Web site (www.naspa.org) is dedicated to brief summaries of institutionally submitted best practices in parent programming. *Partnering with the Parents of Today's College Students*, edited by Kurt Keppler, Richard H. Mullendore, and Anna Carey, was released in 2005 by NASPA. It is topically arranged for use by educators, but also contains an annotated bibliography of resources and some brief descriptions of examples of specific programs.

Other organizations with parental programming and relationship interests include the American College Student Personnel Association, the National Orientation Directors Association, and the National Academic Advising Association. Those organizations' Web sites can be consulted for more information.

The National Resource Center for The First-Year Experience and Students in Transition has published several helpful resources. A new edition of *Empowering Parents of First-Year Students: A Guide for Success*, authored by Richard H. Mullendore and Leslie Banahan, was released in 2007. The 2004 *A Guide for Families of Commuter Students: Supporting Your Student's Success*, by Cathie Hatch and Tracy L. Skipper, was produced in association with the National Orientation Directors Association, and *A Family Guide to Academic Advising*, released in 2003, is written by Donald C. Smith and Virginia N. Gordon. (The Web site for the National Resource Center is www.sc.edu/fye.)

NEW DIRECTIONS FOR HIGHER EDUCATION • DOI: 10.1002/he

There are also a few books aimed at assisting parents with understanding and navigating the college process and their own transition. These include *Letting Go: A Parent's Guide to Understanding the College Years*, by Karen Levin Coburn and Madge Lawrence Treeger (2003), and *Bringing Home the Laundry: Effective Parenting for College and Beyond*, by Janis Brody (2001).

Conclusion

There seems to be broad consensus that the institution-parent relationship is changing, and at its most extreme manifestations presents the helicopter parent phenomenon. But it is important that we not lose sight of the fact that this behavior describes a minority of parents and that it may be the result of institutional failure to provide them adequate information and avenues of appropriate relationship with the campus. Much more common are parents who enter the new territory with lots of questions, lots of concerns, and an earnest, heartfelt intention to be supportive of both institution and student during the many transitions that are part of the collegiate experience. Colleges and universities can make important allies of parents by recognizing their concerns, addressing them with information and guidance on a timely basis, and keeping lines of communication open to give personal attention to individual circumstances.

References

Bickel, R. D., and Lake, P. F. *The Rights and Responsibilities of the Modern University.* Durham, N.C.: Carolina Academic Press, 1999.

Bowden, R. "Evolution of Responsibility: From In Loco Parentis to Ad Meliora Vertamur." *Education*, 2007, *127*, 480–489.

Brody, J. *Bringing Home the Laundry: Effective Parenting for College and Beyond.* Lanham, Md.: Taylor Trade Publishing, 2001.

Coburn, K. L., and Treeger, M. L. *Letting Go: A Parent's Guide to Understanding the College Years.* New York: HarperCollins, 2003.

Colavecchio-Van Sickler, S. "Mommy, Tell My Professor He's Not Nice!" *St. Petersburg Times*, June 19, 2006. Retrieved Feb. 5, 2008, from http://www.sptimes.com/2006/06/19/State/Mommy__tell_my_profes.shtml.

Hatch, C., and Skipper, T. L. *A Guide for Families of Commuter Students: Supporting Your Student's Success.* Columbia, S.C.: National Resource Center for The First-Year Experience and Students in Transition, 2004.

Henning, G. "Is In Consortio Cum Parentibus the New In Loco Parentis?" *NASPA Journal*, 2007, *44*, 538–560.

Keppler, K., Mullendore, R. H., and Carey, A. (eds.). *Partnering with Parents of Today's College Students.* Washington, D.C.: National Association of Student Personnel Administrators, 2005.

Mullendore, R., and Banahan, L. "Designing Orientation Programs." In M. L. Upcraft and others (eds.), *Challenging and Supporting the First-Year Student: A Handbook for Improving the First Year of College.* San Francisco: Jossey-Bass, 2005.

Mullendore, R., and Banahan, L. *Empowering Parents of First-Year College Students: A Guide for Success.* Columbia, S.C.: National Resource Center for The First-Year Experience and Students in Transition, 2007.

National Center for Education Statistics. *Issue Brief: Postsecondary Participation Rates by Sex and Race/Ethnicity, 1974–2003.* Washington, D.C.: U.S. Department of Education, 2005.

Rooker, L. "Presentation to Texas Higher Education Law Conference." Denton, Tex., Apr. 1, 2008.

Smith, D. C., and Gordon, V. N. *A Family Guide to Academic Advising.* Columbia, S.C.: National Resource Center for The First Year of College and Students in Transition, 2003.

Strauss, V. "Putting Parents in Their Place: Outside Class." *Washington Post,* Mar. 21, 2006, p. A8.

MARC CUTRIGHT *is associate professor and director of the Center for Higher Education at the University of North Texas.*

NEW DIRECTIONS FOR HIGHER EDUCATION • DOI: 10.1002/he

5

*Adult students, whether new or returning to higher educa-
tion, experience a unique set of transition challenges. By
understanding the characteristics and needs of this student cohort, colleges and universities are better able to
facilitate adult student success.*

Adult Students in Higher Education: A Portrait of Transitions

Carlette Jackson Hardin

For the past three decades, the face of higher education has been changing
as more and more adult students have entered or reentered college. This
enrollment trend accelerated in the 1970s and early 1980s, when older students, primarily women and part-time students, began to enroll in greater
numbers. The number of college and university students who are twenty-five
years of age and older had increased to 4.9 million by 1987. Enrollment of
students aged forty or older increased 235 percent between 1978 and 1993,
and according to the Council on Adult and Experiential Learning (2000), 43
percent of all students in higher education in 1997 were age twenty-five or
older. Projections are that by 2010, 6.8 million college students will be age
twenty-five or over (National On-Campus Reports, 2002).

Adult students are coming to institutions of higher education for myriad reasons. Many are pursuing their first postsecondary program with the
goal of earning an associate or bachelor's degree. Many of these students will
choose to enroll in community colleges for their first postsecondary
experience as community colleges provide the access, affordability, and con-
venience adults require. As a result, more than half of community college
students are adult students (Frey, 2007).

Other adult students have a college degree and are returning to higher
education to change careers or strengthen their work skills. As baby
boomers retire, many come to higher education with a long-delayed dream
of a first or an advanced degree. Others simply want to learn new skills or
knowledge.

New Directions for Higher Education, no. 144, Winter 2008 © Wiley Periodicals, Inc.
Published online in Wiley InterScience (www.interscience.wiley.com) • DOI: 10.1002/he.325

Adult Student Transitions

Whatever the motivation for enrolling, these students share a common experience: they are all facing one or more transitions in their personal or career life. For some, this transition is viewed positively as they prepare for a new career, advancement, or retirement. For others, the transition comes as a result of a negative life experience. Some have faced corporate downsizing and realize that they cannot compete in the job market without a different or an advanced degree. For these students, attending college classes becomes an additional stressor to that of losing a job and income. Some are in the middle of personal transitions because of a divorce or the loss of a spouse. These students find that in addition to the personal issues that come with such a loss, they are now forced to enter college in hopes of maintaining or improving their life situation. Too often, adults entering or reentering college face the challenge of juggling parenting, job, and school responsibilities. Many are trying to pay for college at the same time they are dealing with a reduction of income.

For many women, the motivation to attend college happens with their changing role in the family. Some are forced to enter college as they face financial difficulties as a result of divorce or the death of a spouse. Some enter after waiting for children to start school or leave home. In most cases, the adult woman returning to college does so to provide support for her family (Allen, 1993).

Whatever the event that triggers an adult student's return to college, it usually constitutes a major life change. When coupled with the added stress of applying, enrolling, and attending classes, adult students often feel disoriented as they confront the transitions. Therefore, while adjusting to the challenges and rigors of college, many adult students are creating new identities in all areas of their lives. In fact, most adult college students are a portrait of life's transitions.

Barriers Facing Adult Students

Adult students are often referred to as nontraditional students, yet not all nontraditional students are adult students. The term *nontraditional* can include traditional-aged students who share common characteristics with their adult counterparts. These characteristics often put them at risk for being unsuccessful. Such characteristics include:

- Delaying enrollment into higher education until adulthood
- Enrolling part time
- Working full time
- Being financially independent
- Being financially responsible for others
- Having family responsibilities
- Having academic deficiencies

NEW DIRECTIONS FOR HIGHER EDUCATION • DOI: 10.1002/he

The National Center for Education Statistics (1996) estimates that over 60 percent of students in U.S. higher education can be characterized as nontraditional. Because of these characteristics, nontraditional students who enter postsecondary education are less likely than their traditional counterparts to attain a degree or remain enrolled after five years (National Center for Education Statistics, 1996). In fact, adult students are most likely to depart from colleges within their first year of enrollment. Therefore, early intervention is needed if adult students are to persist.

The Council on Adult and Experiential Learning (2000) notes that many colleges and universities have struggled to adjust to the changing demographics on their campuses. If adult students are to be successful, colleges must strive to remove the barriers adult students face. In early research on adult students, Pinkston (1987) found that they faced procedural, environmental, psychological, and financial barriers as they pursued a degree. A more recent review found that such barriers fall into four broad categories: institutional, situational, psychological, and educational (Council on Adult and Experiential Learning, 2000; Compton, Cox, and Laanan, 2006; Donohue and Wong, 1997; Hammer, Grigsby, and Woods, 1998; Hardin, 1997; Nordstrom, 1997). These barriers represent issues that threaten the success of adult students and prevent them from meeting their academic, career, and personal goals.

Institutional Barriers. Institutional barriers are college and university policies, procedures, and red tape that hinder the progress of adult students. Often, without realizing it, an institution creates obstacles to students' progress. These might occur any time during a college career, from the moment students consider attending college to the completion of graduation requirements. Madfes (1989) found that when faced with university-imposed barriers, adult students were less tolerant than traditional students and often discontinued their education rather than adding stress to their lives.

Nordstrom (1997) and Hammer, Grigsby, and Woods (1998) found that adult students are focused on completing academic requirements in a minimum amount of time and are primarily concerned with (1) the institution's proximity to home and work; (2) availability of night, weekend, and online courses; (3) extended faculty office hours; (4) quality day care; (5) accurate academic advisement; and (6) quality instruction. Because of the barriers they face, careful academic advisement is essential for adult students. Academic advisers should be selected on the basis of knowledge about and interest in the adult learner. A major key to advising adult students is helping them create realistic long-term goals. According to the Council on Adult and Experiential Learning (2000), the connection between student goals and the path they have selected is not a one-time event conducted at the outset of the academic career. Adult students and their advisers need to continually review and revise what the student wishes to accomplish, what preparations must be made, and how the institution can help the student achieve these goals. Therefore, institutions must select competent and well-trained advisers who are alert to the special problems of adult students.

In the past fifteen years, online courses have been created as one way to reduce institutional barriers, and these courses have provided access to students who never before had a chance to attend college. However, adult students need to be aware that not all online programs are accredited, and some fail to deliver what is promised. As Allen noted in 1993, it is important that students choose to attend the right institution for the right reason. This is more important as new options are created daily. Too often college recruiters are more concerned with enrollment numbers than meeting the needs of the student.

Compton, Cox, and Laanan (2006) stress that colleges need to take a proactive approach to uncovering the needs of adult students rather than waiting for exit interviews of those who are leaving. Many campuses have created offices in which the only focus is to work with adult students. These offices help adult students learn about nontraditional scholarship programs, registration, advising, counseling, career choices, health services, parking, financial aid, housing, networking with other students, and commuting problems, and their staff can answer questions about courses, programs, and instructors.

Situational Barriers. Kerka (1989) describes situational barriers common to adult students such as role conflicts, time management issues, family and work problems, economics, and logistics. Situational barriers cannot be removed by the college or university because they are unique to the individual. Therefore, adult students facing such barriers need services that will smooth their academic adjustment by allowing them to focus on their role as a student. Awareness of the needs and characteristics of adult learners allows institutions to address some of these barriers and improve the transition experience. Lack of financial support, for example, may prevent an adult student from entering or remaining enrolled at the college or university. Eifler and Potthoff (1998) found that finances were a crucial concern of older students. Generally these students are financially independent and have responsibility for others as well. In addition, the financial needs of adult students differ from those of traditional students because of the added costs of housing and child care. Genzuk and Baca (1998) found that adult students are often in low-paying jobs at the time they enter teacher education programs and are afraid of incurring additional debt. Therefore, they might fail to seek the student loans and financial aid available to them. In order to meet these expenses, adult students often continue to work full time while carrying a full course load. For many, this becomes a recipe for disaster.

Because situational barriers can include everything from a lack of affordable housing to a need for legal aid, many institutions have found that an effective way to provide necessary information to returning adult students is through a directory of resources that includes both on- and off-campus organizations. In addition to essential services provided by the college or university, such directories should include information and telephone numbers for church organizations, legal assistance, crisis call lines, safe houses for abused women, and other community services.

The Council on Adult and Experiential Learning (2000) notes that although an increasing number of educators have come to recognize the important role that support services play in the lives of adult learners, the misperception still exists that adult learners are self-supporting and do not need the same level of support as eighteen- to twenty-three-year-old students. In reality, adult learners need at least as much assistance as traditional-aged students, and sometimes more.

Psychological Barriers. Psychological barriers include inadequate coping skills, lack of self-confidence and poor self-image, anxiety about schooling based on prior experience, and negative beliefs or expectations about outcomes (Kerka, 1989). Donohue and Wong (1997) found that adult students were more likely to be at risk for psychological distress than their traditional counterparts and that their needs may be overlooked in a traditional university setting.

In many cases, the adult learner is the first in the family to attend college. Therefore, family support is critical if these students are to succeed. To help secure support from family, social events should be planned for adult students and their families. Adult students should also be encouraged to be more integrated into the social life of the institution. Research shows that students who are more involved in the life of the campus are more likely to persist (National On-Campus Reports, 2002). One way to encourage adult students to participate in campus activities is to include activities for children.

Adult students often go through an identity crisis as they enroll or reenroll in college. Many of these students have neglected their own educational goals while helping spouses or children attain theirs. Other adult students enroll in college after spending years in careers and find it traumatic to be novices after having been successful in their occupations. One adult student maintained that such changes destroy one's ego (Madfes, 1989). Subjects in Madfes's research who began college after a successful career expressed the same feelings of vulnerability as traditional-aged students beginning their first careers after college. Therefore, faculty and advisers must be aware of this issue and work with adult students who are making the transition from being an expert to being a novice.

Adult students often feel isolated on the college and university campus. Eifler and Potthoff (1998) emphasize that cohort groups can help overcome the feelings of isolation that accompany a career change. Nordstrom (1997) found that adult learners easily become isolated from the academic community, and their success depends on opportunities to interact with others who have similar interests and manage multiple roles.

Educational Barriers. Unfortunately, many adult students are not prepared academically. There are numerous reasons for their academic deficiencies. The most common is they sometimes made a decision or decisions that have adversely affected their academic futures. These poor choosers are misprepared rather than underprepared (Hardin, 1997). Typically, poor choosers made decisions that were detrimental to their academic future for one of two reasons. Some poor choosers selected something other than a college preparatory curriculum while they were in high school and therefore are ill prepared for the demands made by the college environment. A second type of poor chooser is the student who dropped out of high school. Many of these students eventually earn a general educational development (GED) diploma and enroll in college with a false sense of security about their academic ability. What they often fail to understand is that a GED measures their ability to complete the most basic of high-school-level work. It does not measure their ability to be successful in college.

Some adult students experience academic difficulties because they have been away from an academic setting for an extended time. Those who have not used skills they learned in high school for several years will find they need practice as they return to college. Some students face academic problems because they have a physical or learning disability, which makes classroom activities a challenge (Hardin, 1997). Many adult learners speak a primary language other than English, and they may struggle to keep up with their classmates.

The Council on Adult and Experiential Learning (2000) notes that the assistance provided to adult students with academic deficiencies is a litmus test for the extent to which the institution is focused on adult learning. Adult-focused institutions provide support so students can hone their academic skills before launching directly into credit-bearing work toward a degree.

Overcoming the Barriers

In spite of the challenges they face, the picture for adult students is not completely bleak. Adult students bring experiences to classrooms that enhance learning for students of any age. Adults are often described by their instructors as more eager, motivated, and committed than their traditional-age counterparts. Faculty are often enthusiastic about teaching these students because of their unique abilities and the richness they bring to the classroom through their diverse backgrounds (Wayne State University, 2000). Once enrolled at a college or university, most adult students say they plan to obtain a degree there.

Knowles (1984) wrote extensively about how adults learn and used the term *andragogy* to describe the art and science of helping adults learn. His basic argument is that adults do not learn in the same way as children and should not be taught in the same manner as children are. Knowles emphasized that adults are self-directed and expect to take responsibility for personal decisions. Adult students want to understand why they need to learn material, and they learn best when they can use the information immediately. Strategies such as case studies, role playing, simulations, and self-evaluation are most useful.

Adult learners recognize and appreciate good teaching (Knowles, 1984). They desire instructors who adopt the role of facilitator or resource rather than lecturer or grader. Therefore, reducing educational barriers for adult students means creating new roles for faculty that include managing and facilitating student learning, not just lecturing or providing direct instruction.

Adult students desire course work that has practical applications. Adults tend to be career focused, and they often value courses and assignments that are relevant to their goals (Allen, 1993). Workplace projects support this concept. Because they must carve out time to study while balancing many roles, they want to know what is expected of them. It is critical that they get feedback early in the term. However, as Imel (1994) notes, a favorite adage of adult educators is that "adult learners vote with their feet." When faced with learning environments that fail to meet their needs, adult students simply stop coming to class.

College and University Interventions

The Council for Adult and Experiential Learning (2000) notes that without good models, colleges and universities will continue to struggle as they serve the growing population of adult students. Based on research at institutions that have been successful working with adult students, the council identified eight principles of effectiveness for serving adult learners. These principles describe processes and approaches that colleges and universities seeking to improve access and quality for adult students can adopt:

> *Outreach.* The institution conducts its outreach to adult learners by overcoming barriers in time, place, and tradition in order to create lifelong access to educational opportunities.
>
> *Life and career planning.* The institution addresses adult learners' life and career goals before or at the onset of enrollment in order to assess and align its capacities to help learners reach their goals.
>
> *Financing.* The institution promotes choice using an array of payment options for adult learners in order to expand equity and financial flexibility.
>
> *Assessment of learning outcomes.* The institution defines and assesses the knowledge, skills, and competencies acquired by adult learners from both the curriculum and life/work experience in order to assign credit and confer degrees with rigor.
>
> *Teaching-learning process.* The institution's faculty uses multiple methods of instruction (including experiential and problem-based methods) for adult learners in order to connect curricular concepts to useful knowledge and skills.
>
> *Student support systems.* The institution assists adult learners by using comprehensive academic and student support systems in order to enhance students' capacities to become self-directed, lifelong learners.

NEW DIRECTIONS FOR HIGHER EDUCATION • DOI: 10.1002/he

Technology. The institution uses information technology to provide relevant and timely information and enhance the learning experience.

Strategic partnerships. The institution engages in strategic relationships, partnerships, and collaborations with employers and other organizations in order to develop and improve educational opportunities for adult learners. (p. 5)

Recognizing the transitional state of adult learners, Frey (2007) notes that the Council on Adult and Experiential Learning recently identified a ninth principle: transitions, described as "supporting guided pathways that lead into and from the institution's programs and services in order to ensure that students' learning will apply usefully to achieving their educational and career goals" (p. 5). In order to help students make the transition to and from their academic programs, the following activities are suggested:

- Create new and expanded course delivery, which includes weekend course offerings and expanded distance education programs.
- Create an adult services office to meet the needs of adult students.
- Redesign Web sites to include information for adult students.
- Redesign traditional orientation sessions to address the unique concerns of adult learners.
- Create programs to assist students with academic deficiencies in the transition to college.
- Create a student mentor or adviser program to help new students negotiate college processes and procedures.
- Form articulation programs between community colleges and universities to promote the smooth advancement of adult students.
- Promote accessibility by providing services at times convenient for adult learners.
- Select and train advisers to work with adult students.
- Form an "adult learner" committee or task force to review issues related to adult students.

Conclusion

For many adult students, returning to college and fulfilling their goals is much like building a house of cards. In order to be successful, each part of their lives must be in place and carefully balanced. When changes occur, whether these changes are created by the student, family, or the institution, this careful balance collapses. Too often, the student then feels that the only option is to drop out. College and university administrators must recognize the needs of this special population and be advocates for adult students. When this occurs, adult learners come to see themselves as capable of handling the transitions of life while becoming lifelong learners.

References

Allen, B. "The Student in Higher Education: Nontraditional Student Retention." *CATA-LYST*, 1993, *23*(3). Retrieved Jan. 21, 2008, from http://scholar.lib.vt.edu/ejournals/CATALYST/V23N3/allen.html.

Compton, J. I., Cox, E., and Laanan, F. S. "Adult Learners in Transition." In F. S. Laanan (ed.), *Understanding Students in Transition: Trends and Issues*, New Directions for Student Services, no. 114. San Francisco: Jossey-Bass, 2006.

Council on Adult and Experiential Learning. *Serving Adult Learners in Higher Education*. 2000. Retrieved Jan. 31, 2008, from http://www.cael.org/pdf/publication_pdf/Summary%20of%20Alfi%20Principles%20of%20Effectiveness.pdf.

Donohue, T. L., and Wong, E. H. "Achievement Motivation and College Satisfaction in Traditional and Nontraditional Students." *Education*, 1997, *119*, 237–244.

Eifler, K., and Potthoff, D. E. "Nontraditional Teacher Education Students: A Synthesis of the Literature." *Journal of Teacher Education*, 1998, *49*, 187–195.

Frey, R. *Helping Adult Learners Succeed: Tools for Two-Year Colleges*. Chicago: Council for Adult and Experiential Learning, 2007.

Genzuk, M., and Baca, R. "The Paraeducator-to-Teacher Pipeline." *Education and Urban Society*, 1998, *31*, 73–88.

Hammer, L. B., Grigsby, T. D., and Woods, S. "The Conflicting Demands of Work, Family, and School Among Students at an Urban University." *Journal of Psychology*, 1998, *132*, 220–227.

Hardin, C. "Who Belongs in Higher Education? A Second Look." In J. Higbee and P. Dwinell (eds.), *Developmental Education and Its Role in Preparing Successful College Students*. Columbia: National Resource Center for The First-Year Experience and Students in Transition, University of South Carolina, 1997.

Imel, S. *Guidelines for Working with Adult Learners*. Columbus, Ohio: ERIC Clearinghouse on Adult, Career, and Vocational Education, 1994. (ED 283 441)

Kerka, S. *Retaining Adults Students in Higher Education*. Columbus, Ohio: ERIC Clearinghouse on Adult, Career, and Vocational Education, 1989. (ED 308 401) Retrieved January 31, 2008, from http://www.ed.gov/databases/ERIC_digests/ed308401.html.

Knowles, M. S. *Andragogy in Action*. San Francisco: Jossey-Bass, 1984.

Madfes, T. J. "Second Careers—Second Challenges: Meeting the Needs of the Older Teacher Education Students." Paper presented at the Annual Meeting of the California Educational Research Association, 1989. (ED 318 713)

National Center for Education Statistics. *Nontraditional Undergraduates: Trends in Enrollment from 1986 to 1992 and Persistence and Attainment Among 1989–90 Beginning Postsecondary Students*. Washington, D.C.: U.S. Department of Education, 1996.

National On-Campus Reports. *An Expert Shares Her Secrets on Programs for Non-Traditional Students*. Report 30, 2002, *14*(3). Madison, Wisc.: Magna Publications, Inc.

Nordstrom, A. D. "Adults Students: A Valuable Market to Target." *Marketing News*, 1997, *31*(19), 20.

Pinkston, R. A. University Support Programs, Academic Achievement, and Retention, 1987. (ERIC. ED 283 441)

Wayne State University. "Bringing Diverse Populations into the Teacher Certification Process." National Conference on Teacher Quality-Exemplary Practices in Teacher Preparation, 2000. Retrieved Jan. 31, 2008, from http://www.ed.gov/inits/teachers/exemplarypractices/b-1.html.

CARLETTE JACKSON HARDIN *is professor of education at Austin Peay State University.*

NEW DIRECTIONS FOR HIGHER EDUCATION • DOI: 10.1002/he

6

*Although the nature of collegiate transition in the sopho-
more year is different from that of first-year students, it is
no less significant or challenging.*

Sophomores in Transition:
The Forgotten Year

Barbara F. Tobolowsky

Over the past several decades, student transitions have become a primary
focus for many higher education staff and faculty. Not surprisingly, these
educators have concerned themselves primarily with the transition into college, because high first-year attrition numbers reflect how challenging this
transition is for many new students. Attention has also been given to the
senior-year transition, because it is the last opportunity institutions have to
ensure that students are adequately prepared for the working world or graduate school. Researchers focus on beginning and ending transitions by
exploring the needs, behaviors, and expectations of both first-year students
and seniors through national and institution-specific surveys such as the
Cooperative Institutional Research Program (CIRP) Freshman Survey and
the National Survey of Student Engagement and by assessing the outcomes
of targeted programs such as first-year and senior seminars.

The same research focus has not been given to the sophomore and
junior years. There is no national instrument that specifically explores student issues and concerns in the middle years of the collegiate experience.
The lack of research on the junior year is particularly striking given the
importance of the junior year in a student's college experience. Tradition-
ally the junior year is the time when students are finally able to focus on
courses in their major, and it is often when students engage in special experiential opportunities such as internships, extended service opportunities,
and study abroad. In addition, these students have the bulk of the leadership responsibilities on many campuses through service as peer leaders,
mentors, and resident advisors. However, given the absence of both research

NEW DIRECTIONS FOR HIGHER EDUCATION, no. 144, Winter 2008 © Wiley Periodicals, Inc.
Published online in Wiley InterScience (www.interscience.wiley.com) • DOI: 10.1002/he.326

and focused campus programs, we leave discussion of the junior year, by necessity, for a later time.

This chapter focuses on the sophomore-year experience, which in the past few years has moved from the background to the forefront for increasing numbers of researchers and campus practitioners. I discuss the unique issues related to the sophomore year, share findings from current research, and conclude with recommendations for those seeking to offer sophomore initiatives or improve those already in existence.

Making the Case for the Importance of the Sophomore Year

Educators should be interested in the sophomore year because this is the year in which students make many of the decisions that help them succeed in subsequent years, such as clarifying their sense of purpose, making major declarations, and narrowing their career options. While some may think that the national conversation about the sophomore year is simply another educational fad, discussion of sophomore issues actually dates back to 1956 when Freedman coined the phrase "sophomore slump." He characterized the second year as one of student inertia and confusion, and contemporary educators note similar behaviors among today's sophomores (Gansemer-Topf, Stern, and Benjamin, 2007).

Some have argued that the significant attention many institutions now give to first-year students has actually made the second year the more difficult transition experience (Scott Evenbeck, personal communication to the author, October 2006). This growing realization that the second year is another potential period of risk for today's college students led the National Resource Center for The First-Year Experience and Students in Transition to publish a monograph that explored the sophomore year (Schreiner and Pattengale, 2000). It was groundbreaking work because it exposed not only the issues for sophomores, but also institutional approaches designed to help them.

In 2005, the National Resource Center, again responding to needs expressed by educators, conducted a study exploring the range of programmatic initiatives that U.S. colleges and universities offer sophomores. That research led to a 2007 monograph that included quantitative findings as well as case studies of exemplary programs from public and private institutions in the United States (Tobolowsky and Cox, 2007).

No one can be sure exactly why, after years of ignoring sophomores, educators became interested in this student population. But perhaps it was the synergy of a number of key dynamics. First, at many private campuses, students develop four-year plans that identify learning outcomes for each of the four years. This focus on each year as a distinct time period in the college experience necessarily shed light on the second year.

NEW DIRECTIONS FOR HIGHER EDUCATION • DOI: 10.1002/he

As private college educators gained awareness of second-year issues, they turned to peer institutions and the National Resource Center for insights regarding programs and supports, which led to conference discussions on sophomores and, in turn, research and publications. This initial movement, led in large part by private institutions such as Beloit College, Colorado College, and Colgate University, encouraged educators at public colleges and universities to turn their attention to sophomores as well. Also, faculty and administrators who saw the success of first-year programs on their campuses found that a focus on second-year students was a natural extension of their earlier efforts. Finally, this more intentional focus on the needs of sophomores may have resulted from institutional concerns about retention: excluding the first year, more students drop out of higher education in the second year than any other year of college (Lipka, 2006).

What is going on that causes second-year students to leave? As with any other departure, the answer is not singular or simple. Freedman (1956) suggested that a "sophomore slump" could be the cause. Students who have not clarified their reasons for attending college or have not selected a major may feel the inertia, confusion, and resulting stress that define the sophomore slump. In addition, courses may become more challenging in the second year as students begin to focus on fields of potential interest. They feel a greater investment in these courses than in some of the first-year general education courses that seemed unrelated to their desired career. This greater investment raises the stakes for students, resulting in added pressure and stress (Coburn and Treeger, 2003; Evenbeck, Boston, DuVivier, and Hallberg, 2000; Freedman, 1956). In more recent research, sophomores discussed feeling "invisible" and "lost." These students felt they were not getting the support they need to make the critical decisions they must make in their second year (Gansemer-Topf, Stern, and Benjamin, 2007).

Other researchers have investigated both previous and current student development theories to see if any of the extant theories might shed light on second-year students. Lemons and Douglas (1987) noted that four of Chickering's vectors (1969) explain the issues of sophomore students: developing competence, moving through autonomy toward interdependence, establishing identity, and developing purpose. Baxter Magolda (1992) found that sophomores tended to fall in earlier stages of intellectual development (that is, absolute knowing and transitional knowing). Most recently Schaller (2005) developed a four-stage model based on interviews she conducted with sophomore students at four-year institutions. This model directly relates to the students' process of making a decision on a major: moving from random exploration through focused exploration and tentative choices to commitment.

Thus, as sophomores' voices are heard and as faculty, administrators, and staff recognize the needs of these students, various initiatives have been created to address those needs. These efforts run the gamut from social activities to more academic ones, but each represents this new focus on the sophomore transition.

Findings of the National Survey of Sophomore Initiatives

In 2005, as a way to better understand institutional efforts, the National Resource Center for The First-Year Experience and Students in Transition conducted a national survey of sophomore initiatives. All regionally accredited private and public four-year institutions were sent an e-mail message inviting them to participate in the Web-based survey. The response rate was 33.5 percent, with 382 institutions participating in the survey.

The survey questions addressed the types of initiatives offered, their administrative homes, and any assessment conducted evaluating the effectiveness of the initiatives. The survey found that sophomore programs are often new and have not been subjected to assessment. Seldom did institutions describe comprehensive approaches to the second year. Rather, they either offered distinct programs that might focus exclusively on sophomores or programs designed for all students in which sophomores were encouraged to participate.

The most common institutional efforts directed at sophomores are those focused on career planning (74.2 percent), major selection (65.3 percent), and academic advising (61 percent). This seems appropriate in that sophomores are often required to declare their majors during or at the end of the sophomore year. Institutions also provide engagement opportunities for sophomores through class events such as trips, dinners, and dances (46.3 percent); student government (38.7 percent); service-learning or community service (32.8 percent); and cultural events such as plays, musical events, and multicultural fairs (18.8 percent). There are also efforts to engage students academically through special credit-bearing courses geared to sophomores (31.4 percent) and opportunities to coteach, mentor, or assist in teaching a class (20.7 percent).

Campus efforts described by survey respondents are designed to address one or more of the following five goals: creating a sense of community, fostering social engagement, facilitating faculty-student interaction, encouraging major and career exploration, and promoting academic engagement and leadership.

A Sense of Community. Some institutions offer publications geared specifically toward their second-year students (16.8 percent) to help create a unique class identity. These publications might take the form of newsletters, Web sites, or brochures. Regardless of their form, all provide information on events and deadlines of particular interest to sophomores. At Drew University, students and parents are sent a letter from the dean acquainting them with events specific to careers, as well as information regarding offices that might assist students in selecting a major. The

University of Denver has a second-year Web site that includes information about a half-day reorientation conference and other programs, as well as frequently asked questions about registration, internships, advising, and other topics.

Efforts to build community do not stop at publications. Beloit College has offered a long-running sophomore retreat to help second-year students establish a sense of community. Macalester College holds the Sophomore Fiesta, and Colorado College hosts the Sophomore Luau with the primary objective of building a collective identity. Other institutions go beyond campus events and offer class trips to achieve this goal. Both Washington and Lee University and Colgate University host sophomore trips to Washington, D.C. New York University uses the vast resources of the city to engage students with trips to local museums. These initiatives, which vary greatly, are all intended to engage students and build community.

Social Engagement. Often second-year students begin to question the relationships they developed during the first year and seek new, healthy relationships with their peers (Schaller, 2005). Many social and academic opportunities, including retreats (Beloit College, Grinnell College) and peer mentoring (University of Rhode Island), help students connect with other students. Other sophomore-specific initiatives that foster social engagement include curricular learning communities (Emory University, Texas Tech University, Colorado College), a lecture series (Colgate University), trips (Emory, Washington and Lee University), dances (Rowan University, Saint Anselm College), and dinners or other special meals (Yale University, Loyola College, St. Lawrence University). All of these experiences expose second-year students to new peer groups and encourage them to develop meaningful relationships with other students.

Student-Faculty Interaction. Many researchers (Astin, 1993; Kuh and Hu, 2001) have reported the benefits of student-faculty interaction both in and outside the classroom. This survey also found that campuses are creating situations that encourage these interactions. For example, faculty often serve as mentors to sophomore students (31.4 percent) to encourage student-faculty interaction outside the classroom. At Bennington College, for instance, three faculty members from different disciplines, as well as the student's faculty adviser, meet with the student several times throughout the student's college career to review and revise their four-year plan. This process ensures ongoing student-faculty interaction.

Major and Career Exploration. Major and career exploration is clearly the main goal of the sophomore year, and many of the initiatives offered are geared to help students in decision making in these areas. In addition to career and major fairs, which are common on many campuses, some institutions offer other unique programs. West Virginia University sponsors the Sophomore Outdoor Adventure Reorientation (SOAR) program, a one-week spring or summer outdoor adventure trip that focuses on helping students explore and determine their majors. The residential colleges at Yale University have special sophomore advising nights, when the college dean and residential students discuss how to choose a major.

As students turn their attention to career development and major selection, self-assessments are a natural part of that inquiry. Students need to know their interests and goals before they make those decisions. The Career Services Office at Asbury College provides self-assessment as part of the career advising program to help sophomores select their major. Because many sophomore students are questioning their identity and sense of meaning and purpose, opportunities for self-assessment and reflection can prove to be extremely beneficial as students make their initial, if not final, career and major decisions.

Academic Engagement and Leadership. Campuses also seek to encourage students' intellectual development in the sophomore year. One approach that Beloit College and Colorado College use is to provide venture grants to sophomores that enable them to explore their areas of interest. For instance, Beloit offers the grants to support the students "to travel, do research, start a business, something they always wanted to do" but lacked the resources. Other campuses have service-learning requirements that help students see the world outside themselves. One of the key outcomes of service-learning is to make students better citizens and encourage them to reflect on their own identity. Benedict College requires sophomores to complete twenty hours of service each semester, with the goal of students' "putting their learning into action and honing their leadership skills."

Several institutions engage students academically by offering credit-bearing courses for sophomores. At Emory University and Rhodes College, these courses are part of the core requirements; at Austin College, a sophomore course focuses on leadership development. Several institutions provide opportunities for sophomores to coteach or assist in teaching that not only develop leadership potential but also help engage them academically. At Willamette University, sophomore students can serve as teaching assistants in the first-year seminar course, and at the University of Rhode Island, students coteach the seminar. These classroom experiences help students gain leadership skills as well as academic expertise.

Students have other noncourse-based leadership opportunities during their second year. Furman University offers leadership training, while Butler University, Austin College, and the State University of New York at Fredonia have sophomore class officers who provide the sophomore voice in campuswide discussions or plan second-year-focused events. Sophomore programming is wide ranging, addressing both the academic and social development of students.

Recommendations

Research (National Resource Center, 2005) finds that an emphasis on sophomores is a new programming area for many institutions. Although sophomores deserve attention and efforts, the task of providing more programming and assistance seems daunting with resources that are already stretched. Here are seven steps for creating or improving sophomore initiatives (Tobolowsky and Cox, 2007):

Do not work alone. Begin to seek out others on campus who are interested in sophomore issues. Many movements begin as grassroots efforts, so search out like-minded colleagues. In addition, try to get higher administration's buy-in, because if programs are part of institutional long-range planning, they will be ensured financial support.

Take stock of the current situation. Taking stock has two primary steps. First, talk to students to determine their needs and concerns. Then conduct a campus audit to identify what is being offered. This may sometimes require serious investigation because these programs are rarely housed in one office. However, much can be learned from this process. Sometimes programs that work well for a small subset of students (perhaps a mentoring program for sophomores interested in science) will be good for the entire class. An audit of existing programs developed for sophomores may lead to reorganizing the offerings under one office or appointing a director of second-year programs.

Develop second-year traditions. The process of developing traditions provides students an opportunity to reestablish relationships, form new ones, and feel that they matter and belong. These events can include welcome-back events prior to the start of the second year, a sophomore common reading or lecture series, or a dance or other social gathering for second-year students. Ideally, campuses should offer a number of second-year events that engage sophomores academically and socially.

Provide career and major exploration events. These events help students accomplish what is perhaps the most critical issue of the sophomore year: declaring a major and thinking about career decisions. They can include major and career information fairs or requiring sophomores do self-assessments to assist them in the decision-making process.

Communicate to sophomores. One of the most telling findings from the National Survey of Sophomore Initiatives was that having a second-year newsletter (electronic or hard copy) was a relatively easy and inexpensive way to communicate events of interest to sophomores. Communication shows students they matter, and it lets them know about events or activities of special interest.

Provide good advising for sophomores. We know that "good advising is the single most underestimated characteristic of a successful college experience" (Light, 2001, p. 81). Since most institutions want their students to be able to declare their majors by the end of the sophomore year, the importance of advising cannot be overstated.

Assess the impact of all programs and activities. Research speaks volumes to higher education administrators. Be sure to include assessment as an element in the development of every program and initiative; only then will you know how to improve or build on your efforts.

Conclusion

Clearly the sophomore transition is important because of the several critical decisions students must make in their sophomore year. In the past, in spite of their importance, sophomores have been neglected as campuses focused their efforts primarily on first-year and senior students. Recently researchers and practitioners have started to look at sophomores as a unique cohort and have uncovered the transition issues tied to the second year. This chapter shares some of those findings to illuminate institutional responses to second-year issues. In most cases, campuses offer ad hoc or piecemeal programs rather than comprehensive, holistic, and assessed initiatives that address second-year students' academic and social needs and assist them in their transition through college.

Lessons learned from the success of many first-year and senior initiatives can be applied to initiatives designed for the sophomore year. The most important lesson is this: a comprehensive approach to the sophomore year, embedded in campus culture and tied to the campus mission, is more likely to yield broad institutional support and long-term sustainability than a fragmented approach. This chapter provides educators the information they need to help move sophomores from the shadows into positions of greater visibility within colleges and universities.

References

Astin, A. W. *What Matters in College? Four Critical Years Revisited.* San Francisco: Jossey-Bass, 1993.

Baxter Magolda, M. B. *Knowing and Reasoning in College.* San Francisco: Jossey-Bass, 1992.

Chickering, A. W. *Education and Identity.* San Francisco: Jossey-Bass, 1969.

Coburn, K. L., and Treeger, M. L. *Letting Go.* New York: HarperCollins, 2003.

Evenbeck, S. E., Boston, M., DuVivier, R. S., and Hallberg, K. "Institutional Approaches to Helping Sophomores." In L. A. Schreiner and J. Pattengale (eds.), *Visible Solutions for Invisible Students: Helping Sophomores Succeed.* Columbia: University of South Carolina, National Resource Center for The First-Year Experience and Students in Transition, 2000.

Freedman, M. B. "The Passage Through College." *Journal of Social Issues,* 1956, *12*(4), 13–28.

Gansemer-Topf, A. M., Stern, J. M., and Benjamin, M. "Examining the Experiences of Second-Year Students at a Private Liberal Arts College." In B. F. Tobolowsky and B. E. Cox (eds.), *Shedding Light on Sophomores: An Exploration of the Second College Year.* Columbia: University of South Carolina, National Resource Center for The First-Year Experience and Students in Transition, 2007.

Kuh, G., and Hu, S. "The Effects of Student-Faculty Interaction in the 1990s." *Review of Higher Education,* 2001, *24*, 309–332.

Lemons, L. J., and Douglas, R. R. "A Developmental Perspective of Sophomore Slump." *NASPA Journal,* 1987, *24*(3), 15–19.

Light, R. *Making the Most of College: Students Speak Their Minds.* Cambridge, Mass.: Harvard University Press, 2001.

Lipka, S. "After the Freshman Bubble Pops: More Colleges Try to Help Their Sophomores Thrive." *Chronicle of Higher Education,* Sept. 8, 2006, p. A34.

National Resource Center for The First-Year Experience and Students in Transition. *National Survey of Sophomore-Year Initiatives.* Columbia: University of South Carolina, National Resource Center for The First-Year Experience and Students in Transition, 2005.

Schaller, M. A. "Wandering and Wondering: Traversing the Uneven Terrain of the Second College Year." *About Campus,* July–Aug. 2005, pp. 17–24.

Schreiner, L. A., and Pattengale, J. (eds.). *Visible Solutions for Invisible Students: Helping Sophomores Succeed.* Columbia: University of South Carolina, National Resource Center for The First-Year Experience and Students in Transition, 2000.

Tobolowsky, B. F., and Cox, B. E. (eds.). *Shedding Light on Sophomores: An Exploration of the Second College Year.* Columbia: University of South Carolina, National Resource Center for The First-Year Experience and Students in Transition, 2007.

BARBARA TOBOLOWSKY *is associate director of the National Resource Center for The First-Year Experience and Students in Transition and clinical faculty member in the University of South Carolina's College of Education.*

NEW DIRECTIONS FOR HIGHER EDUCATION • DOI: 10.1002/he

Since transfer students are a fact of undergraduate life today, institutional faculty and staff members need to be aware of the issues affecting their transition and strive to make it as successful as possible.

"Feeling Like a Freshman Again": The Transfer Student Transition

Barbara K. Townsend

Undergraduate transfer is a fact of life. At least 40 percent of students attend more than one institution on their path to a baccalaureate degree (Adelman, 2005). Some students initially attend a two-year college, so transfer is to be expected if they seek a baccalaureate. Among the students in the Beginning Postsecondary Students Longitudinal Study 1995–2001 (BPSLS:95/2001), over 40 percent of those who started postsecondary education in a public two-year school in 1995 transferred at least once by June 2001. Two-year college students are not the only ones who transfer. The same BPSLS:95/2001 data also show that 27 percent of students who started at a public four-year school and almost 24 percent who started at a private, nonprofit school transferred at least once (National Center for Education Statistics, 2002). Some of this transfer may include what is known as "reverse transfer," or transferring to a community college after attending a four-year college or university (Townsend, 1999).

As a result, there is increasing interest in transfer students' transition to their new institution, often referred to as the receiving institution. In this chapter, I describe the two parts of the transfer transition: the transfer process itself, which I label transfer transition part 1, and the adjustment once at the receiving institution, which I call transfer transition part 2. To do so, I draw primarily from my current research about transfer students' experiences once at their receiving college or university. I conclude with suggestions for ways that administrators and faculty at both the sending and receiving campuses can facilitate the transfer student transition.

NEW DIRECTIONS FOR HIGHER EDUCATION, no. 144, Winter 2008 © Wiley Periodicals, Inc.
Published online in Wiley InterScience (www.interscience.wiley.com) • DOI: 10.1002/he.327

The basis for this chapter's description of transfer students' experiences is several qualitative studies conducted at a large, public, research extensive, midwestern university. This university's undergraduate student body consists primarily of full-time, traditional-age students drawn to the school partly because it exemplifies the stereotypical collegiate experience, including Division I athletic teams, an extensive Greek presence, and the requirement that all first-year students live on campus. Several years ago, nineteen community college transfer students at this university were individually interviewed (see Townsend and Wilson, 2006, for details). Two years later, a follow-up study of these students was conducted with eleven of those still on campus (see Townsend and Wilson, in press). Results of these two studies are used here, along with results from several focus groups conducted in 2007.

Students in the focus groups were selected in two ways. One set of students had enrolled in a one-credit course developed as part of an institutional effort to retain transfer students. This optional course about being a transfer student, whether from a two-year or four-year institution, is offered by several of the university's colleges or disciplines (for example, business, education, psychology). Students in the course are considered to be part of a transfer student interest group (TRIG). Several of the TRIGs agreed to participate in a focus group about the transfer process and about being a transfer student. The questions asked were a variant of those asked of the students in the two transfer studies. Responses of the thirty-seven students from four TRIGs were taped and then transcribed for later analysis. In addition, leaders of one TRIG asked that their nine students receive the questions and individually respond to them in writing, which they did.

The second way students responded through focus groups was by means of a provost-driven effort to learn how transfer students perceived their experiences at the institution, including the transfer process itself, and how the university could improve the transfer process and services for transfer students. Using essentially the same questions as those used with the TRIG students, institutional faculty and staff interviewed twenty-seven community college transfer students who responded to an invitation for "pizza and conversation" (Barnes, 2007, p. 1). When they arrived, they were placed in small groups of two to four students. Their comments were recorded by hand and then compiled into a master list of responses categorized by the questions asked.

In other words, responses of seventy-three students from the 2007 focus groups, as well as nineteen students from the previously described studies (Townsend and Wilson, 2006, in press) inform most of the remarks in this chapter. From these responses of almost a hundred students, several themes emerged. The themes are divided into comments about the transfer process itself and about transfer students' experiences after enrollment at the receiving institution.

NEW DIRECTIONS FOR HIGHER EDUCATION • DOI: 10.1002/he

The Transfer Process, or Transfer Transition Part 1

The transfer process encompasses the steps students take to move from their current or sending institution to their receiving one: deciding where to transfer, applying to that college or university, and receiving the institution's decision about their admission, which may include indicating which credits will transfer.

In deciding where to transfer, students are influenced by a number of factors that likely influenced their decision to attend their initial institution. These factors include how much it will cost to attend, how far the campus is from their home, and whether any of their friends or relatives are at the possible receiving college or university. Each of these factors may also influence the college-choice decision of a native student at the institution. However, an additional and distinctive factor for transfer students is the extent to which their already accumulated college credits will transfer or be accepted at the receiving institution. While first-time college students may be concerned about whether and how many of their dual enrollment or dual credit courses or advanced placement courses will be accepted, they took these courses prior to their college attendance. Transfer students, of course, are already college students who have earned course credits while in college. They want all of these credits to transfer; otherwise, they believe their college tuition money and time have been wasted.

Once potential transfer students have decided where to apply, they must go through the college application process. Transfer students bring to this process prior experience in applying to a college. This process typically includes filling out an institution's application form (usually an online one now), arranging for their transcripts to be sent to the institution, and paying an application fee. Students may also seek institutional forms of financial aid.

For potential transfer students, another important part of the application process is learning how many and which credits a college or university will accept. Sometimes this information is available through institutional Web sites detailing institutional articulation agreements or through state-level Web sites describing articulation agreements for a state's public and sometimes its private institutions. However, information about articulation agreements for courses and programs is not always so accessible. Thus, at times students apply to and decide to go to an institution without knowing in advance if all of their previously earned college credits will be accepted and, if they are accepted, in what way they will count toward a particular major's requirements.

In terms of transfer transition part 1, the student voices heard in this study were almost uniform in expressing why they chose the university in the study. The majority selected it because of a particular major, which makes sense for transfer students. Many of them already have all or most of their general education courses completed and are ready to take courses in their major. Some transfer students also wanted to come to this university because they had family members or friends who were graduates or were currently attending it. Cost was rarely mentioned except when a student had a parent who worked at the university, thus entitling the student to a significant tuition discount. Several of the students also chose this university because they wanted the stereotypical college experience of living in a residence hall, belonging to a sorority or fraternity, attending intercollegiate athletic events, and generally enjoying campus life.

Completing the application was frustrating for some, who complained that the application process took weeks or even a couple of months, while others indicated they had completed the process quickly. Perhaps the differences stem from the time of year students submit an application (some times are busier than others) and the care with which students completed the application, including having the requisite information on hand. A related frustration was the uncertainty about how much financial aid they would receive and the difficulty of getting the financial aid application through the institution's system. Interestingly, students did not complain about having to complete the Free Application for Federal Student Aid, perhaps because they had already experienced completing it prior to attending their initial institution.

As might be expected for transfer students, by far the most frequent frustration in the application process was the transfer of course credits. Most of the students did not say that they had lost course credits, but that may be because many of the two-year college transfer students had completed the associate of arts (A.A.) degree before transferring. The A.A. degree is commonly designated as the transfer degree and is designed to articulate with the first two years of students' general education requirements. At the university described here, students who earn an A.A. degree with a 2.5 grade point average (GPA) or above are accepted as juniors. However, the most common complaint (20 percent of the students) was frustration with the number of prior credits accepted that would count toward the desired major or still not knowing how many or which of their courses had transferred. At this institution, students receive a general acceptance into a particular college, like the College of Arts and Science, but are not automatically accepted into the major of their choice. Only after they are admitted to a college can they apply to a program or department within it. Typically it is not until students are accepted into their major and meet with an adviser that they learn how many of their courses count and in what way (as electives, general education courses, or major courses). Adviser meetings usually do not occur until after a student has matriculated and may not occur during the first semester if the student does not take the initiative to set up a meeting.

Transfer Transition Part 2

Once students have been accepted at the institution of their choice and decide to transfer there, they begin the second part of the transfer transition:

NEW DIRECTIONS FOR HIGHER EDUCATION • DOI: 10.1002/he

becoming a student at the receiving institution. To a certain extent, this part of transfer transition begins with the campus's official orientation program, which may or may not include a specific orientation for transfer students. At this university, orientation is known as Summer (or Winter) Welcome and is designed for beginning first-year university students. There is also a Transfer Day for transfer students. However, transfer students can choose to attend Summer/ Winter Welcome in lieu of Transfer Day. After orientation, transfer transition part 2 continues as students select and attend their first classes and seek to connect academically with faculty and socially with students on their new campus or institutional home.

Just as transfer students are experienced in the application process, they also bring experience as college students. Thus, they are unlike beginning first-year students in that they have already survived college life and shown they can succeed in an academic environment. Perhaps as a result, the dominant theme that emerged from the studies described in this chapter was that transfer students, whether they transferred from a community college or four-year school, "feel like a freshman again" in their lack of knowledge about how their new school works (for example, where students can and cannot park and under what conditions, where to go for course advising). Yet transfer students were explicit about not being first-year students and did not want to be treated like them. Transfer students' desired differential treatment included not rooming with freshmen because these students were just learning how to be college students, whereas transfer students already know how to be college students, although not yet at their new institution. In addition, the students in these focus groups and interviews perceived that as transfer students, they had different interests from first-year students. As one transfer student said, "I get back to my dorm at night and my freshman roommate just wants to go out partying, night after night. I'm past that." Similarly, another said, "There's a big difference between eighteen and twenty. You do a lot of growing up after the first year of college."

In adjusting to their new institution, those who had transferred from small campuses, especially community colleges, initially found the large size of the campus and the faculty's impersonal attitude somewhat daunting. Some community college transfers indicated they were not used to the apparent lack of interest of faculty in knowing who their students were or whether they came to class. Community college transfers were also more likely than four-year college transfers to indicate they had to stretch to meet this university's academic expectations. In these comments, community college students are indicating some of the factors—institutional size, faculty attitudes toward students, and academic expectations—that contribute to what is known as "transfer shock" (Hills, 1965), a much documented phenomenon that typically results in a lowered GPA the first semester on campus.

Occasionally a transfer student already has some friends or a family member at the receiving institution, in which case the social adjustment is easier than for individuals who do not know another soul on campus.

NEW DIRECTIONS FOR HIGHER EDUCATION • DOI: 10.1002/he

However, both sets of students are faced with having to find and make friends in a place where most students' friendships have already been formed, usually in the freshman year. This situation holds true for both two-year and four-year college transfer students.

None of the transfer students expressed a sense that they were not wanted on campus, although in some institutions, community college transfers are not viewed positively. Given some people's negative perceptions of the community college, students who transfer from it are sometimes devalued (Berger and Maloney, 2003). Four-year college transfer students apparently do not face this challenge; at least it has not been documented in the admittedly small literature about four-year college transfer students.

Suggestions for Facilitating the Transfer Transition

Suggestions for facilitating the transfer transition are categorized in terms of student suggestions emerging from the focus groups and interviews and my suggestions building on those of students, yet addressed at a more general institutional level. Since only two-year colleges have the formal mission of preparing students for transfer, suggestions for what sending institutions can do to facilitate the transfer transition will be aimed at two-year colleges.

Student suggestions about what receiving institutions can do to facilitate the transfer transition reflect the nature of the receiving institution's student body. In the university in this chapter, its transfer transition efforts are framed within a primary focus on full-time, traditional-age students seeking a traditional collegiate experience. Many of the transfer students at this institution want this experience, as reflected in their suggestions as to what the institution can do to smooth their transition. Suggestions from students at a college or university where the majority of students are part-time commuter students, often with family responsibilities, would likely vary in some respects.

Transfer Transition Part 1. Students had few suggestions about how to improve the transfer process itself. Their one suggestion regarding financial aid was for more scholarships for transfer students. Four-year college transfer students were most vocal about this because no institutional scholarships were available to them, whereas community college students who transferred with an A.A. degree were eligible for some institutional aid. Students simply wanted all aspects of the application process, including the determination of financial aid and the acknowledgment of which credits would transfer and in what categories, to work smoothly and quickly.

At the two-year college or sending-institution level, students need to understand in advance of their transfer that some of their credits may not transfer. Understanding in advance is preferable to frustration when they arrive on campus and learn, for example, that the general statistics course they took at their prior college will not count in lieu of the required statistics for agricultural education students. Thus, two-year colleges can and should partner with the four-year colleges or universities to which the bulk of their students transfer. The partnership can include efforts to develop a joint or co-admission process to facilitate early admissions, and efforts to develop programmatic articulation agreements so that community college students will know while at the two-year school which general education courses are appropriate for their intended major at the four-year school. Programmatic agreements, while time-consuming to develop, are a critical means to lower student frustration over the failure of prior earned credits to count toward their degree.

Not just administrators but also two-year and four-year college faculty need to work together on the articulation agreements. Faculty at two-year colleges need to understand the expectations of four-year college or university faculty in specific courses to ensure that the two-year college course will indeed prepare the transfer student for upper-division course work. Similarly, four-year faculty need to meet their two-year colleagues and feel confident that what two-year college students are learning will prepare them well for course work at the four-year institution.

Transfer Transition Part 2. Within the context of wanting to be treated as transfer students, not first-year students, transfer students wanted a Summer Welcome or orientation geared to them as transfer students. At the same time, some wanted elements of the freshman orientation in their orientation. For example, some wanted the opportunity to stay overnight instead of just having a half-day or one-day orientation. Students also suggested having other transfer students tell them about the campus and what they had done to adjust socially and academically to it. These same people could also serve as mentors to new transfer students. At the department level, students suggested that during the orientation, there could be a department reception for transfer students or a faculty dinner for all transfer students to demonstrate that faculty cared about these students. Both commuter and residential transfer students wanted a transfer orientation that emulated the one for freshmen by providing lots of opportunities for the students to get to know one another and form connections that will last beyond the orientation.

As another manifestation of not wanting to be treated like freshmen, transfer students who lived on campus suggested having a residence hall just for transfer students or perhaps a floor within each residence hall. Similarly, they wanted to room only with other transfer students, not with freshmen. Commuter transfer students wanted differentiation of their status by having a parking lot just for commuter transfer students and priority in receiving parking lot assignments.

Student suggestions to facilitate further academic and social adjustment at the receiving institution included having more TRIGs by departmental major. One student commented about walking into her first large class and seeing students grouped by their Greek membership or their freshman interest group membership. She suggested that being in a TRIG was a way to have a sense of small group membership. Having more TRIG students would create a sense of a cross-campus TRIG community. This sense of community could be enhanced by having an end-of-the-semester party of all the TRIGs.

Several of the suggestions transfer students had for ways the institution could help them adjust socially included ways transfer students could meet one another besides in TRIGs. For example, there could be contact groups or even formal organizations especially for transfer students who are parents or who work full time or commute. The underlying assumption seemed to be that fellow transfer students would be seeking friends and thus would be more welcoming and friendlier than native students.

From an institutional perspective, it is important to concentrate on what a specific college or university can do to facilitate its transfer students' transition, whether this is a transition from the sending institution or to the receiving institution. To determine what its transfer students need, institutional faculty and staff need to ascertain the students' specific issues and concerns and suggestions for improvement. Focus groups and individual interviews, the methods used to gather the information in this chapter, are important means of ascertaining students' perceptions of their experiences and can provide helpful information.

In ascertaining students' transfer transition needs, it is also important to distinguish between issues affecting any college student's needs versus the needs and issues unique to transfer students. For example, almost all students, undergraduate and graduate, at this university complain about the parking situation; there simply are not enough parking spots to accommodate all the students, and many are a mile or more away from the campus. Similarly, almost all of the institution's new students (first-year, transfer, and graduate students) complain about not understanding where to park and under what conditions. Thus, parking frustrations are a shared student experience, cutting across class year and transfer status. While students can suggest increased parking spaces to facilitate their experience as transfer students, it is unlikely that this institution can or will heed this suggestion. However, it could do a better job of helping students to understand in advance of the first day of classes where to park and under what conditions.

Among issues unique to transfer students at the receiving institution, it is important to distinguish between issues unique to four-year-college transfer students versus two-year-college transfer students. For example, both groups of transfer students wanted more scholarships, but four-year-college transfer students were particularly frustrated about the lack of scholarships, because some had given up institutional scholarships at their sending institution to attend this university, which has no institutional aid for four-year-college transfers.

In short, institutional efforts at facilitating transfer transition should be based on the needs of their particular transfer students. Both two-year and four-year school faculty and staff should seek student advice as to how to improve both parts of the transfer transition.

Conclusion

Transfer students are experienced college goers. They have already gone through the college application process at least once before beginning another application process in order to transfer. They have also been students at another college or university before going to their receiving institution, so they know how to be college students. However, at their new institution, they may "feel like a freshman again," because they need to learn how to be students in a new place. They need to learn how the new campus operates bureaucratically, academically, and socially (Poisel and Stinard, 2006).

Their adjustment time is probably shorter than that of first-year students and can certainly be facilitated by institutional efforts to ease their transition. Whatever the extent and nature of transfer students in an institution's student body, campus leaders must commit to smoothing their transition and helping them move successfully through the period of "feeling like a freshman again."

References

Adelman, C. "Moving into Town—and Moving on: The Community College in the Lives of Traditional-Age Students." Washington, D.C.: U.S. Department of Education, 2005.

Barnes, T. "Summary of Responses from Focus Group Questions of Currently Enrolled MU Transfer Students (Former Community College Students)." Unpublished manuscript, Oct. 2007.

Berger, J. B., and Maloney, G. D. "Assessing the Transition of Transfer Students from Community Colleges to a University." *NASPA Journal*, 2003, *40*(4), 1–23.

Hills, J. R. "Transfer Shock: The Academic Performance of the Junior College Transfer." *Journal of Experimental Education*, 1965, *33*, 201–215.

National Center for Education Statistics. *Descriptive Summary of 1995–96 Beginning Postsecondary Students: Six Years Later*. Washington, D.C.: U.S. Department of Education, 2002.

Poisel, M. A., and Stinard, C. A. "Networks for Transfer Success." *Journal of Applied Research in the Community College,* 2006, *12,* 139–146.

Townsend, B. K. (ed.). *Understanding the Impact of Reverse Transfers on Community Colleges*. New Directions for Community Colleges, no. 106. San Francisco: Jossey-Bass, 1999.

Townsend, B. K., and Wilson, K. B. "'A Hand Hold for a Little Bit': Factors Facilitating the Success of Community College Transfer Students." *Journal of College Student Development*, 2006, *47*, 439–456.

Townsend, B. K., and Wilson, K. B. "The Academic and Social Integration of Persisting Community College Transfer Students." *Journal of College Student Retention*, in press.

Barbara K. Townsend *is professor of higher education and director of the Center for Community College Research at the University of Missouri-Columbia.*

8

The last of the formal undergraduate transitions is the one out of college and back to either the "real world" or graduate or professional study. The senior year transition embodies both opportunities and challenges for students and institutions.

Institutional Efforts to Move Seniors Through and Beyond College

Jean M. Henscheid

The portrait of the American college senior is a mix of economic pressures and shifting choices. The pot at the end of the rainbow, higher salaries and independence, sits next to "loan payment due" notices and ever changing "help wanted" lists. Student excitement about leaving college is tempered with understandable feelings of uncertainty. This graduating senior says it best: "I am most worried about knowing what I'll be doing with my 'real' life. For the past four years I've known exactly what to do and where I should be. That doesn't mean I'm not ready to be done with school, though" (Theresa Martinez, personal communication to the author, May 1, 2008). Understanding that the senior year represents another critical transition point for college students, many U.S. colleges and universities are taking intentional steps to help students bring closure to their collegiate experience and accomplish the final undergraduate transition successfully.

In this chapter, I consider the senior experience in its entirety, beginning with definitions of the senior year and the senior year experience (SYE), data on who among American students makes it to the final year, what the majority of them are studying, how much debt they are leaving with, and the overall advantages of a college education. I then revisit the curricular landscape of the senior year with a summary of findings from a national survey on senior seminars and capstone courses, and I provide examples of senior year programs found in American colleges and universities. The chapter ends with recommendations for practitioners on enhancing and integrating all components of the senior experience and for researchers on ways to broaden understanding about this experience.

New Directions for Higher Education, no. 144, Winter 2008 © Wiley Periodicals, Inc.
Published online in Wiley InterScience (www.interscience.wiley.com) • DOI: 10.1002/he.328

Definitions and Dimensions of the Senior Experience

Because the standard for completing an undergraduate degree is no longer four years, the definition of a senior as a "college student in the process of completing the final quarter of the baccalaureate degree" (Gardner, Van der Veer, and Associates, 1998, p. 4) seems more appropriate than the more traditional description of a senior as a student in the fourth undergraduate year. The broader definition allows inclusion of the growing number of students who matriculate into and out of two or more institutions, those who stop out for one or more academic terms, and those enrolled in programs that require more than four years for completion. As seniors, students move through experiences in the curriculum and cocurriculum that culminate their years as undergraduates. When these experiences are intentionally designed to "promote and enhance greater learning and satisfaction and a more successful transition" (p. 12), they qualify under Gardner and Van der Veer's definition of the *senior year experience*.

Once students complete their senior year and graduate, nearly 60 percent intend to move back in with their parents, according to the 2004 edition of the MonsterTRAK Annual Entry-Level Job Outlook—a survey of college students, recent graduates, and prospective employers (Kennedy, 2004). More than half of the 1,092 survey respondents also reported that they did not expect a job offer by graduation (compared to 23 percent in 2001), and 16 percent were continuing on to graduate school, thereby postponing entry into a tight job market.

Degrees in business were the first choice for American college students who graduated in 2004–2005 (312,000 of the 1.4 million degrees conferred). The next largest numbers of degrees were granted in social sciences and history (157,000) and education (105,000). While several fields, including physical sciences, health professions, and engineering, have seen up and down fluctuations since the mid-1990s, other fields, such as visual and performing arts, religion, journalism, and leisure studies, have enjoyed a more than 20 percent increase in numbers of degrees conferred (U.S. Department of Education, 2007). How well these degree aspirations match with the next decade's employment outlook is mixed. According to the U.S. Department of Labor (2008), professional and service positions will see the fastest percentage growth, at more than 15 percent each.

Students who graduate prepared for one type of position and make a job change after graduation are likely to make that change, and several more, if the behavior of American workers remains consistent. Respondents to the National Longitudinal Survey of Youth 1979 held an average of 10.5 jobs from ages eighteen to forty, with men holding 10.7 jobs and women holding 10.3 jobs (U.S. Department of Labor, 2006).

As college graduates move into the workforce, employers are mostly satisfied that they are prepared for entry-level positions but are concerned that students may not be ready for higher-level jobs, according to results of a survey conducted for the Association of American Colleges and Universities (AAC&U) and released in January 2008 (Peter D. Hart Research Associates). Survey respondents indicated that colleges and universities have equipped students well in teamwork, ethical judgment, intercultural skills, social responsibility, quantitative reasoning, and self-knowledge. But at least three in ten employers give college graduates low scores for their preparedness in global knowledge, self-direction, writing, critical thinking, and adaptability.

Among college graduates, women are the majority and are the faster-growing segment. In the 2002–2003 year, women earned some 58 percent of all degrees, 60 percent of associate degrees, 58 percent of bachelor's degrees, and 59 percent of master's degrees (U.S. Department of Education, 2005).

Earning a first bachelor's degree in 1999–2000 among individuals who had not stopped out of college for six or more months took fifty-five months (four and a half years). Students who transfer from one institution to another took longer to complete their degrees than students who attended only one institution (fifty-nine months compared to fifty-one months), and students who attended three or more institutions on average took sixty-seven months (five and a half years). Students attending private institutions during this period completed their degrees about six months faster than students attending public institutions (fifty-seven versus fifty-one months; U.S. Department of Education, 2003).

Once students receive their bachelor's degrees, they are likely to earn incomes up to 60 percent higher than those with just high school diplomas (U.S. Department of Education, 2006), with income levels varying by major field (Horn and Zahn, 2001; Thomas and Zhang, 2005). These higher salaries are covering the accumulated debt on college tuition rates that have tripled in the past twenty years (American Credit Counselors, 2006). According to the U.S. Department of Education (Toppo, 2005), these tuition rates and changes in loan policies have resulted in a dramatic increase in the number of students borrowing money for college. Greg Toppo, reporting on a U.S. Department of Education study in 2005, noted that the average undergraduate borrowed $19,300 from all sources to attend college compared to $12,100 a decade earlier. Students' major fields determine how much of their incomes will go toward repaying these debts; the highest-paid graduates pay just 5 percent of monthly salaries toward loans, and the lowest paid use 15.4 percent of monthly earnings to pay off college debt (Toppo, 2005).

In terms of nonmonetary quality-of-life issues, Pascarella and Terenzini (2005) conclude from their analysis of studies conducted in the 1990s that college graduates typically have a greater sense of well-being than their nongraduating counterparts. They are more involved in their communities (including increased civic and political involvement) and are typically healthier, as are their children.

In sum, a high percentage of today's college graduates are female, graduating after more than four years of college, often intending to return to their parents' homes, and carrying nearly $20,000 in debt. While business and education continue to be the degrees of choice among many college students, major fields with less obvious direct ties to professional preparation are becoming increasingly attractive. Once they obtain their degrees, college graduates typically enjoy a higher quality of life when compared to nongraduates and can anticipate changing jobs at least ten times by age forty. According to employers, college graduates are self-aware and socially aware ethical team players but lack skills in global knowledge, self-direction, writing, critical thinking, and adaptability.

Efforts to Support Seniors

In 2000, the National Resource Center for The First-Year Experience and Students in Transition published the results of a national survey of senior seminars and capstone courses in *Professing the Disciplines* (Henscheid, 2000). In this volume, I argued that individual academic disciplines are exclusive owners of the student's senior year of college and that by the time most students become seniors, their experience of campus community is limited. Their friendships are likely to be with a subset of like-minded individuals enrolled in academic major-focused courses, their mentors will probably be individual faculty who teach those courses, and their activities are primarily concentrated on finishing the degree.

I was partly right. Individual departments, not whole institutions, primarily own the academic lives of senior students. However, a broader look at the senior year, beyond the courses students take, reveals that a range of other staff and faculty are responsible for what happens outside the major. Although across U.S. colleges and universities, responsibility for the senior year is shared, my research indicates that at individual institutions, a small faction is typically designated to take charge of these efforts. Generally the senior year experience is not characterized by the kind of cross-functional collaboration educators now recognize as necessary for creating a student's successful first college year (Kuh and others, 2005; Upcraft, Gardner, and Barefoot, 2005).

Institutional efforts to help seniors through and out of their final college experiences and prepare them for a complex world fall under five types: senior seminars and capstone courses, programs to prepare students for their careers, opportunities for students to make intellectual connections across course work, events that celebrate the achievement of becoming a college senior, and activities that work toward cohesion among the senior class and alumni.

Senior Seminars and Capstone Courses. Major findings of the 1999 National Survey of Senior Seminars and Capstone Courses (Henscheid, 2000) indicated that the curricular centerpiece of the senior year is most often a course intended to cap off the academic major and prepare students for work in related fields. More than 70 percent of respondents reported that senior seminars and capstone courses are discipline or department based. A few of them help students make intellectual links across disciplines, and even fewer share priorities with nonclassroom programs, including preparing students to make life choices, improving their life skills, and making career plans. The primary goals of most senior seminars and capstone courses, as prioritized by about 75 percent of survey respondents, are to foster integration and synthesis within the academic major, promote integration and connections between the academic major and the work world, and improve seniors' discipline-specific career preparation and preprofessional development. Less than 2 percent of respondents indicated that their senior seminars or capstone courses were intended to address personal adjustment issues seniors may encounter in their transition out of college.

Programs to Prepare Students for Careers. Outside of senior seminars and capstone courses, colleges and universities focus much of their attention in the senior year on preparing students for careers. Components of the Senior Year Experience at Minnesota State University Moorhead, for example, include careers, personal finance, wellness, workplace ethics, leadership, transitions, dress for success, and etiquette. Bridgewater State College in Massachusetts offers a three-part, semester-long program that assists students in the transition from college to work. Resources address business dining etiquette, dressing for success, evaluating job offers, negotiating salaries, relocating, surviving the first job, managing finances, and buying or leasing a car. A senior exposition offers an opportunity to gather graduation regalia, order class rings, and pick up alumni information. Graduating students also have an opportunity to network with alumni using a "speed dating" approach. Saint Louis University's senior year program, called "Disorientation," instructs students on landing a dream job, financial basics, the first day of work, and dining etiquette.

Programs That Provide the Opportunity for Students to Make Intellectual Connections Across Course Work. A second type of senior experience program asks students to reflect on and synthesize the content of their course work in either the academic major or across courses. For example, Allegheny College has used a senior project that allows students to showcase academic achievements since the senior capstone experience was created in 1821. The project integrates disciplinary knowledge with skills honed in courses throughout the students' years at the institution and provides students the opportunity to reflect on skills needed for their professions.

The Senior Year Experience at Otterbein College offers seniors the opportunity to integrate learning from the academic major, the college's integrative studies program, and elective courses. Saint Louis University offers a senior legacy symposium that showcases students' academic accomplishments and leaves the institution with a tangible contribution of the student's work. Monmouth College (Illinois) asks students to build on their past studies to address important social issues through individual and group projects. The intent is to funnel students' energies into planning for lives of productive citizenship.

Programs Celebrating the Achievement of Becoming a College Senior. In their 1997 book on the senior year experience, Gardner and Van der Veer encouraged institutions to use the final quarter of the undergraduate years in part to acknowledge the accomplishments of their seniors through symbols, dinners, ceremonies, and other events. Bridgewater State College uses its Senior Expo to allow students to gather important information about participating in a number of special class events. The Alumni Association and College Advancement Office of Cornell College work with a class agent to organize celebration activities for the senior class. During a five-year term that starts in the senior year, class agents attend alumni association board of directors meetings and perform other duties on behalf of their senior class. Colorado College celebrates its senior class by having it adopt a theme that exemplifies its values and attitudes. The 2007–2008 theme, "Would you like fries with that?" celebrated the attitude of this class that students should move beyond conformity and embrace the role of global change agent.

Programs That Work Toward Cohesion Among the Senior Class and Alumni. The celebratory activities and events are also an opportunity to connect members of the senior class to each other, and in some instances, the institution is frank about increasing new alumni donations. At Lynchburg College, the senior class campaign committee is organized to ask seniors to pledge their support to the institution's annual fund. Pledges in annual increments of twenty-five dollars are made over four years and come due the year after graduation. Columbia University offers similar advice to seniors about staying connected to their alma mater through an e-community, e-mail forwarding, and ongoing career counseling. Cornell College asks the class agent to write two letters to classmates each year of their five-year term, offering news and information and, once per year, seeking donations to the college.

Cross-Campus Collaborations. Individual campus departments are typically responsible for senior experience programs across all five types. Career development and placement units take lead roles in senior year experiences emphasizing those transitional needs. Alumni relations offices are often responsible for the celebratory and community-building activities, and academic units drive senior thesis and creative projects that are a culmination of the students' intellectual activities. On campuses where more than one senior experience program exists, more than one unit or division is involved. Responsibility for Saint Louis University's services for seniors crosses multiple offices: alumni, career development, Disorientation, the senior legacy symposium, and financial services. At Wartburg College the senior year experience is a collaborative effort between Residence Life and the Pathways Center, which houses academic advising, major exploration services, and graduate and professional school and career-related opportunities. Students assume the lead for a portion of senior activities on some campuses, including Lynchburg, Colorado, and Barnard colleges.

In sum, the five types of senior experience programs currently offered are organized to help students prepare for their careers and adult responsibilities, reflect on and synthesize course work in the major or across courses, celebrate the accomplishment of completing the bachelor's degree, and build personal connections among classmates intended to transcend graduation. Individual departments or units are most often responsible for design and delivery of senior year experiences.

What Senior Year Experience Programs Say About Institutional Values

The heavy burden of securing a job to begin the long process of paying off college loans is a centerpiece of today's senior experience. The emphasis many institutions place on helping their graduating students find vocational success suggests that they see themselves as direct providers of support for first-time professional job seekers. This role sometimes frustrates academic faculty, who view their responsibility as providing students a liberal education that transcends career preparation (Knight Abowitz, 2006). In her 2006 *About Campus* article, Knight Abowitz suggested, however, that the educators' role is not to dissuade students from seeing college as a path to a career. It is their role to help students see the larger purpose in their academic work. By the same token, the institution's obligation is not to convince faculty members that they must prepare students for a career. It is their obligation to demonstrate connections between liberal education and a student's gainful employment after college.

Senior experience programs reviewed for this chapter do address students' intellectual and vocational needs, but often not together. When they are combined in senior seminars and capstone projects, they are most often confined to major-related vocations. The American penchant for changing jobs more than ten times by the age of forty suggests that broadening the conversation is in order. While colleges and universities may be doing well in helping seniors land a first job (related to the major), the evidence suggests that more may need to be done to explicitly link the skills they have learned throughout college with the skills they will need for their second, third, fourth, and tenth jobs. The good news, according to Knight Abowitz (2006), is that the skills of a liberal education are the ones that mobile workers need.

Allegheny College's seniors are offered the opportunity to make an explicit link between liberal learning across courses in and outside the major and the world of work. The portfolio required of George Mason University's New Century College seniors is the ideal place for students to demonstrate how liberal learning, work, and life skill development are linked. Through these and other venues for reflection and synthesis, students can demonstrate to themselves and others where and how the liberal learning needed to be a mobile worker has been developed. Emphasis in this area would begin to address the concerns of employers, including the respondents to the AAC&U survey (Peter D. Hart Research Associates, 2008), who indicate that college graduates are ready for their first jobs but lack skills most needed later, including adaptability, critical thinking, writing, global knowledge, and self-direction. The skills may be there, but opportunities to demonstrate these skills for external assessment may not be. A review of programs for this chapter revealed that many institutions have yet to turn this period toward assessment, identified by Schilling and Schilling (1998) as critical in the senior year. Reflection on and synthesis of liberal learning and learning for the world of work would seem to be a logical centerpiece of this assessment.

This advice to turn the seniors more toward reflection on and synthesis of liberal learning is based on three untested assumptions. The first is that the ten or more jobs Americans move through by the time they are forty probably will not be directly or closely related to their academic majors. If all jobs are major related, perhaps that fact would justify the narrow focus of most senior seminars and capstone courses. The second assumption is that the respondents to the AAC&U survey (Peter D. Hart Research Associates, 2008) are representative of all employers who hire America's college graduates. The accuracy of this assumption would, of course, require further investigation. And the third is that opportunities for reflection and synthesis are probably not currently offered in most major-linked senior seminars. Assessment could test the validity of that assumption; however, assessment is often such an afterthought or so deeply embedded that it remains hidden, even from the most prying eyes.

Conclusion

American colleges and universities do much to prepare seniors for life during and after the final quarter of their undergraduate experience. They help them apply for jobs, make final intellectual connections, celebrate achievements, and build a sense of community within the senior class. The demands of working for a lifetime suggest that more should be done. In other words, we seem to have succeeded in preparing students for their entry-level jobs; the work now is to succeed in preparing them for what comes next.

References

American Credit Counselors. "Average American Credit Card Debt." Houston: American Credit Counselors, 2006. Retrieved Mar. 9, 2008, from http://www.americancredit.org/Average-American-Credit-Card-Debt.html.

Gardner, J. N., Van der Veer, G., and Associates. *The Senior Year Experience: Facilitating Integration, Reflection, Closure, and Transition.* San Francisco: Jossey-Bass, 1998.

Henscheid, J. M. *Professing the Disciplines: An Analysis of Senior Seminars and Capstone Courses.* Columbia: University of South Carolina, National Resource Center for The First-Year Experience and Students in Transition, 2000.

NEW DIRECTIONS FOR HIGHER EDUCATION • DOI: 10.1002/he

Horn, L. J., and Zahn, L. *From Bachelor's Degree to Work: Major Field of Study and Employment Outcomes of 1992–93 Bachelor's Degree Recipients Who Did Not Enroll in Graduate Education by 1997.* Washington, D.C.: U.S. Department of Education, National Center for Education Statistics, 2001.

Kennedy, D. G. "Eureka!" *American Demographics,* June 1, 2004. Retrieved Mar. 9, 2008, from http://findarticles.com/p/articles/mi_m4021/is_5_26/ai_n6077841.

Knight Abowitz, K. "The Interdependency of Vocational and Liberal Aims in Higher Education." *About Campus,* Apr.–May 2006, pp. 16–22.

Kuh, G. D., and others. *Student Success in College: Creating Conditions That Matter.* San Francisco: Jossey-Bass, 2005.

Pascarella, E. T., and Terenzini, P. T. *How College Affects Students: A Third Decade of Research.* San Francisco: Jossey-Bass, 2005.

Peter D. Hart Research Associates. "How Should Colleges Assess and Improve Student Learning? Employers' Views on the Accountability Challenge. A Survey of Employers Conducted on Behalf of the Association of American Colleges and Universities." Washington, D.C.: Peter D. Hart Research Associates, 2008. Retrieved Mar. 12, 2008, from http://www.aacu.org/advocacy/leap/documents/2008_Business_Leader_Poll.pdf.

Schilling, K. L., and Schilling, K. M. "Looking Back, Moving Forward: Assessment in the Senior Year." In J. N. Gardner, G. Van der Veer, and Associates (eds.), *The Senior Year Experience: Facilitating Integration, Reflection, and Transition.* San Francisco: Jossey-Bass, 1998.

Thomas, S. L., and Zhang, L. "Post-Baccalaureate Wage Growth Within Four Years of Graduation: The Effects of College Quality and College Major." *Research in Higher Education,* 2005, 46(4), 437–459.

Toppo, G. "College Graduates See Their Debt Burden Increase." *USA Today,* Mar. 27, 2005. Retrieved Mar. 9, 2008, from http://www.columbia.edu/cu/news/clips/2005/03/28/collegeUSATODAY.pdf.

U.S. Department of Education, National Center for Education Statistics. *The Condition of Education 2003, Indicator 21.* Washington, D.C.: U.S. Department of Education, 2003.

U.S. Department of Education, National Center for Education Statistics. *Postsecondary Institutions in the United States: Fall 2003 and Degrees and Other Awards Conferred: 2002–03.* Washington, D.C.: U.S. Department of Education, 2005.

U.S. Department of Education, Institute of Education Sciences, National Center for Education Statistics. *The Condition of Education 2006.* Washington, D.C.: U.S. Department of Education, 2006.

U.S. Department of Education, National Center for Education *Statistics Digest of Education Statistics, 2006.* Washington D.C.: U.S. Department of Education, 2007.

U.S. Department of Labor, Bureau of Labor Statistics. *Number of Jobs Held, Labor Market Activity, and Earnings Growth Among the Youngest Baby Boomers: Results from a Longitudinal Survey.* Washington D.C.: U.S. Department of Labor, 2006. Retrieved Mar. 12, 2008, from http://www.bls.gov/news.release/pdf/nlsoy.pdf.

U.S. Department of Labor, Bureau of Labor Statistics. "Percent Change in Total Employment by Major Occupational Group, Projected 2006–2016." In *2008–2009 Occupational Outlook Handbook.* Washington D.C.: U.S. Department of Labor, 2008. Retrieved Mar. 12, 2008, from http://www.bls.gov/oco/images/ocotjc06.jpg.

Upcraft, M. L., Gardner, J. N., and Barefoot, B. O. (eds). *Challenging and Supporting the First-Year Student: A Handbook for Improving the First Year of College.* San Francisco: Jossey-Bass, 2005.

Jean M. Henscheid *is the director of the core curriculum at the University of Idaho and executive editor of* About Campus.

New Directions for Higher Education • DOI: 10.1002/he

9

While this volume has defined and explored the common elements of collegiate transition, there are layers of complexity in students' characteristics and educational pathways that make this transition experience different for every student.

Collegiate Transitions: The Other Side of the Story

Betsy O. Barefoot

This volume of *New Directions for Higher Education* has explored collegiate transitions by focusing on students as they experience the higher education continuum, beginning before the first year of college and continuing through graduation. The chapters have reviewed the characteristics of today's students and their parents, as well as recent changes in the pathways many students take through higher education. While it is tempting to think about the various stages of higher education as relatively predictable time periods within a four-year trajectory, we must remember that the real world is not nearly so neat and tidy. This concluding chapter explores the many murky areas between and within transition periods that challenge our attempts to generalize about student experiences. The chapter also considers the differences among individual students that sometimes make it difficult to categorize them accurately according to age and stage.

The exploration of collegiate transitions in this volume begins with two chapters that call into question historic notions about when the transition from high school to college starts. David Conley in Chapter One and Nancy Hoffman, Joel Vargas, and Janet Santos in Chapter Two maintain that if students are to succeed and ultimately graduate, their transition to higher education should commence well before they enter a college or university as official freshmen. As more and more high schools and colleges blend curricula and even merge facilities, the first-year student is becoming increasingly difficult to identify and label.

Jennifer Keup in Chapter Three and Carlette Jackson Hardin in Chapter Five introduce the issues related to traditional and nontraditional

NEW DIRECTIONS FOR HIGHER EDUCATION, no. 144, Winter 2008 © Wiley Periodicals, Inc.
Published online in Wiley InterScience (www.interscience.wiley.com) • DOI: 10.1002/he.329

students. However, given the nature of today's college students, the lines between these demographic categories are becoming increasingly blurred. Today in both four-year and two-year institutions, many traditional-aged students have nontraditional responsibilities such as parenting, working full time, or being financially independent. In all respects except their age, these eighteen- to twenty-one-year-old students are having a nontraditional college experience.

Marc Cutright focuses in Chapter Four primarily on parents who are supportive of and involved (or overly involved) in their son's or daughter's college experience. However, there are other parents and families who are indifferent or even hostile toward the whole idea of college. Such attitudes often stem from a lack of understanding about college life or from fear that college students will reject family culture or mores. But whether they are too involved or hostile, the attitudes of parents and families can affect the degree to which students make a successful transition to college.

As Jean Henscheid notes in Chapter Eight on the senior year, the four-year baccalaureate degree no longer represents the reality for many students. Because of part-time attendance, occasional changes in major, transfer between institutions, or the common pattern of "stopping out" of college, students may spend five, six, or even more years completing an undergraduate degree. Whether as a function of age or life experience, students who complete a four-year degree in six or eight years will likely experience the senior year transition differently than four-year graduates do.

The lengthening of time to degree often begins in the first year. Many first-year students attend part time, and others, whether at four-year or two-year institutions, make the transition to college in a year or more of developmental or preparatory course work. Students who take more than a year to complete the first-year curriculum complicate our notions of not only what it means to be a first-year student but also what it means to be a sophomore. Barbara Tobolowsky explores in Chapter Six the developmental tasks that we typically associate with the sophomore year, but some students who have either lingered in the first year or stopped out for a period of time may have moved beyond the need to clarify purpose or settle on a major, the archetypal tasks of the sophomore year.

The simple act of determining who is considered a transfer student has become a challenge for institutions as well as for state systems, many of which have their own official definitions with various delimiting specifications. Barbara Townsend focuses in Chapter Seven on the most common type of transfer experience: the vertical transfer from a two-year to a four-year institution. But other students make lateral (four-year to four-year or two-year to two-year) or reverse (four-year to two-year) transfers, some may "swirl" between multiple campuses, and increasing numbers are concurrently enrolled at more than one campus. These varied patterns make study of the common aspects of student transfer difficult and call into question the assumptions practitioners sometimes make about the characteristics and needs of transfer students.

To create a full picture of student transitions, it is also important to recognize the importance of particular events and decision points that can be sprinkled throughout the undergraduate experience. The City University of New York (2005) calls these "critical junctures" and suggests that educators provide special support to students at these specific points in time. CUNY's Office of Academic Affairs acknowledges that many of these junctures are institution specific but lists others that are generally common to the undergraduate experience:

- Passing institutional tests or entrance examinations
- Passing progression examinations or examinations for entrance into graduate or professional school
- Passing gateway courses
- Declaring or changing majors
- Moving in and out of developmental education
- Moving in and out of English as a Second Language curricula

While CUNY focuses its definition of critical junctures on academic situations, even nonacademic crises, such as a rejection from a desired fraternity or sorority or an athletic team, are events that might distract students from their academic work and negatively affect their academic momentum and willingness to be fully invested in the college experience.

Taken as a whole, the chapters in this volume provide solid evidence that colleges and university educators care about, and provide support for, student transitions. To date, however, educators have focused most of this support on the transition captured in the term *first-year experience*. In fact, in the United States today, almost all colleges and universities offer some sort of special initiative to facilitate the transition of first-year students (Policy Center on the First Year of College, 2002). Educators are just beginning to realize, however, that support beginning when students step on campus for the first time and ending when they reach the sophomore year is not enough. We must do a better job of looking back to the way students are prepared for college by their high school and family experiences, and we also need to expand our efforts by looking forward to monitor student progress throughout the undergraduate years.

During the years of collegiate transition, it is the rare student who sails through without occasionally floundering, going in the wrong direction, or even capsizing. And that is where we as higher education professionals come in. As "transition guides," many college and university educators employ available research as well as their prior experiences with students to make predictions about the kinds of support and assistance that today's and tomorrow's students will need. Then they use their knowledge and experience to develop institutional initiatives that focus transitional assistance where it is most likely to be needed.

While our assumptions and predictions are a valuable starting point, they must be tempered by the realization that students and patterns of college attendance are changing rapidly, and often unpredictably. The diversity of students, coupled with the many pathways of college attendance, require that we go beyond assuming that all students within a certain stage of transition need the same type of assistance. Rather, we need to view and respond to students as individuals. Whether students are in their first year, middle years, or final year of college, each has unique needs, both academic and personal, and each will experience a unique transition trajectory.

Providing targeted transition assistance to individual students is not easy and cannot be done on the cheap. Assistance at this level requires that we develop close relationships with each student. Firsthand knowledge about students' academic, social, and personal needs and experiences requires time, dedicated personnel, creativity, and, inevitably, resources. But as educators who are committed to providing quality learning experiences in an atmosphere of support, this is our challenge as we go forward.

Many high schools, colleges, and universities have in place a range of successful programmatic efforts to support students and their families as they experience collegiate transition. And there is no doubt that both collectively and individually, these institutional efforts are making a positive difference for numbers of students. In spite of our successes, we have the opportunity to make an even bigger difference by joining forces with other educators at all levels of the educational pipeline. Through working together, we can develop a fuller understanding of how to respond effectively to common transition needs as students move along their educational journey. In addition, we can deepen our understanding of the unique experiences of individual students so that more of them will make successful transitions into, through, and out of a college or university with the all-important associate or baccalaureate degree in hand.

References

City University of New York. *Board of Regents Statewide Plan for Higher Education in New York State, Appendix A,* Jan. 28, 2005. Retrieved June 9, 2008 from http://www.highered.nysed.gov/Quality_Assurance/statewideplan/page6.htm.

Policy Center on the First Year of College. "Second National Survey of First-Year Academic Practices." 2002. Retrieved June 10, 2008, from http://www.firstyear.org/survey/survey2002/index.html.

BETSY BAREFOOT *is codirector and senior scholar in the Policy Center on the First Year of College located in Brevard, North Carolina. She is also a fellow in the National Resource Center for The First-Year Experience and Students in Transition at the University of South Carolina.*

NEW DIRECTIONS FOR HIGHER EDUCATION • DOI: 10.1002/he

INDEX

Academic behaviors, 9–10
Academic knowledge and skills, 8–9
Accelerated learning options, 16–25
Adelman, C., 16, 69
Adult students, challenges facing, 49–56
Allen, B., 50, 52, 55
Andragogy, 54
Antonio, A., 4, 10
Aspengren, K., 5
Astin, A. W., 63

Baca, R., 52
Banahan, L., 43, 44, 46
Barefoot, B. O., 2, 28, 82, 89, 92
Barnes, T., 70
Baxter Magolda, M. B., 61
Benjamin, M., 60, 61
Berger, J. B., 74
Bickel, R. D., 40, 41
Boston, M., 61
Bowden, R., 41
Bowers, C. J., 3
Bransford, J. D., 10
Brody, J., 47
Brooks, D., 27, 28
Brown, A. L., 10

Carey, A., 46
Cassidy, R. C., 29
Chickering, A. W., 61
Clark, B., 32
Cleary Act of 1990, 41
Coburn, K. L., 47, 61
Cocking, R. R., 10
Colavecchio-Van Sickler, S., 39
College Knowledge, 8
College knowledge, description of, 4, 10
College Now, 19–21
College readiness: academic behaviors
  and, 9–10; conclusions on, 11–12;
  defined, 3–4; facets of, 6–7; key
  cognitive strategies for, 7–8; self-
  management and, 9–10
College students: adult, 49–56; seniors,
  79–86; sophomores, 59–66;
  traditional-aged, 27–35; transfer
  students, 69–77

College versus high school, 4–6
Collegiate transitions, complexity of,
  89–92
Coltrane, G., 23
Compton, J. I., 51, 52
Conley, D. T., 1, 3, 4, 5, 7, 8, 10, 13, 89
Copeland, R. E., 4
Cox, B. E., 60, 65
Cox, E., 51, 52
Crissman Ishler, J. L., 28, 30
Cureton, J. A., 30, 34
Cutright, M., 1, 39, 48, 90

Donohue, T. L., 51, 53
Douglas, R. R., 61
Dual enrollment pathways, 17–21
Dual enrollment programs, 16–17
DuVivier, R. S., 61

Early college schools, 18, 21–24
Eifler, K., 52, 53
Evenbeck, S., 60, 61

Family Educational Rights and Privacy
  Act (FERPA), 40–41, 43, 45–46
Foster, K., 21, 22, 23
Freedman, M. B., 60, 61
Frey, R., 49, 56

Gallagher, R. P., 30, 31
Gansemer–Topf, A. M., 60, 61
Gardner, J. N., 28, 80, 82
Genzuk, M., 52
Goldberger, S., 15, 16
Gordon, V. N., 46
Gray, E., 7
Greico, E. M., 29
Grigsby, T. D., 51

Hallberg, K., 61
Hammer, L. B., 51
Hardin, C., 2, 49, 51, 54, 57, 89
Harper, C. E., 29
Hatch, C., 46
Health Insurance Portability and
  Accountability Act, 41, 45
Henning, G., 34, 41

Henscheid, J. M., 2, 79, 82, 87, 90
Higbee, J. L., 4
Hills, J. R., 73
Hipp, S., 4
Hoffman, N., 1, 15, 18, 25, 89
Horn, L. J., 81
Howe, N., 27, 28
Hu, S., 63
Hurtado, S., 27, 30, 32, 33

Imel, S., 55
Interpretation, as cognitive strategy, 7

Jobs, preparing college seniors for,
    80–82, 83, 85–86
Jones, S. R., 28
Junco, R., 33

Karp, M. M., 19–21
Keeling, S., 27, 28
Kennedy, D. G., 80
Keppler, K., 46
Kerka, S., 52, 53
Keup, J. R., 1, 27, 37, 89
Kirst, M., 4, 10
Kitzrow, M. A., 30, 31
Knight Abowitz, K., 85
Knowles, M. S., 54, 55
Koch, A. K., 28
Korn, W. S., 27
Kuh, G., 63, 82

Laanan, F. S., 51, 52
Lake, P. F., 40, 41
Lang, J. A., 32
Learn & Earn schools, 23–24
Lemons, L. J., 61
Levine, A., 30, 34
Light, R., 65
Lipka, S., 61
Lundell, D. B., 4

Madfes, T. J., 51, 53
Maloney, G. D., 74
Martinez, T., 79
McEwen, M. K., 28
McGaughy, C., 7
Meade, T., 18, 19
Mental and emotional health of stu-
    dents, 29–31
Michalowski, S., 21
Millennials, defined, 27–28. See also
    Traditional-aged students

Mullendore, R. H., 43, 44, 46
Multiculturalism, 28–29

Nakkula, M., 21, 22, 23
Newton, F. B., 27, 28
Nordstrom, A. D., 51, 53

Orientation, 43–44, 73, 75

Parents, as valued partners, 39–47
Pascarella, E. T., 81
Pattengale, J., 60
Perrine, R. M., 31
Pinkston, R. A., 51
Poisel, M. A., 77
Potthoff, D. E., 52, 53
Pritchard, M. E., 31
Problem solving, 7
Pryor, J. H., 27, 30, 32, 33
Purpose of college, redefining, 31–33

Readiness, college: academic behaviors
    and, 9–10; conclusions on, 11–12;
    defined, 3–4; facets of, 6–7; key
    cognitive strategies for, 7–8; self-
    management and, 9–10
Reasoning, 7
Ritchhart, R., 9
Robbins, S. B., 10
Rooker, L., 45
Root, M. P., 29

Saenz, V. B., 27, 30, 32, 33
Santos, J., 1, 15, 19, 25, 89
Schaller, M. A., 61, 63
Schneider, C. G., 33
Schreiner, L. A., 60
Self-management, 9–10
Seniors, college, 79–86
Sharkness, J., 27
Skipper, T. L., 46
Smith, D. C., 46
Sophomore Outdoor Reorientation
    (SOAR) program, 63
Sophomores in transition, 59–66
Stern, J. M., 60, 61
Stinard, C. A., 77
Stout, O., 5
Strauss, V., 39
Strauss, W., 27, 28
Students: adult, 49–56; college seniors,
    79–86; college sophomores, 59–66;

traditional-aged, 27–35. *See also*
  Transfer students
Study skills, 10
Subcultures, student, 32

Technology in college environment, 33–35
Terenzini, P. T., 81
Thomas, S. L., 81
Time management, 10, 41
Tobolowsky, B., 2, 59, 60, 65, 67, 90
Toppo, G., 81
Townsend, B., 2, 69, 70, 77, 90
Traditional-aged students, 27–35
Transfer students, 69–77
Treeger, M. L., 47, 61
Trow, M., 32

Upcraft, M. L., 28, 82

Van der Veer, G., 80
Vargas, J., 1, 15, 23, 25, 89
Veach, D., 5
Venezia, A., 4, 10

Wilson, G. S., 31
Wilson, K. B., 70
Wong, E. H., 51, 53
Woods, S., 51

Zahn, L., 81
Zhang, L., 81

NEW DIRECTIONS FOR HIGHER EDUCATION

ORDER FORM SUBSCRIPTION AND SINGLE ISSUES

DISCOUNTED BACK ISSUES:

Use this form to receive 20% off all back issues of *New Directions for Higher Education*.
All single issues priced at **$23.20** (normally $29.00)

TITLE	ISSUE NO.	ISBN

Call 888-378-2537 or see mailing instructions below. When calling, mention the promotional code JB9ND to receive your discount. For a complete list of issues, please visit www.josseybass.com/go/ndhe

SUBSCRIPTIONS: (1 YEAR, 4 ISSUES)

☐ New Order ☐ Renewal

U.S.	☐ Individual: $89	☐ Institutional: $228
CANADA/MEXICO	☐ Individual: $89	☐ Institutional: $268
ALL OTHERS	☐ Individual: $113	☐ Institutional: $302

Call 888-378-2537 or see mailing and pricing instructions below.
Online subscriptions are available at www.interscience.wiley.com

ORDER TOTALS:

Issue / Subscription Amount: $ _____

Shipping Amount: $ _____
(for single issues only – subscription prices include shipping)

Total Amount: $ _____

SHIPPING CHARGES:
First Item $5.00
Each Add'l Item $3.00

(No sales tax for U.S. subscriptions. Canadian residents, add GST for subscription orders. Individual rate subscriptions must be paid by personal check or credit card. Individual rate subscriptions may not be resold as library copies.)

BILLING & SHIPPING INFORMATION:

☐ **PAYMENT ENCLOSED:** *(U.S. check or money order only. All payments must be in U.S. dollars.)*

☐ **CREDIT CARD:** ☐ VISA ☐ MC ☐ AMEX

Card number _____ Exp. Date _____

Card Holder Name_____ Card Issue # _____

Signature _____ Day Phone _____

☐ **BILL ME:** *(U.S. institutional orders only. Purchase order required.)*

Purchase order # _____
Federal Tax ID 13559302 • GST 89102-8052

Name_____

Address_____

Phone_____ E-mail_____

Copy or detach page and send to: **John Wiley & Sons, PTSC, 5th Floor**
989 Market Street, San Francisco, CA 94103-1741

Order Form can also be faxed to: **888-481-2665**

PROMO JB9ND

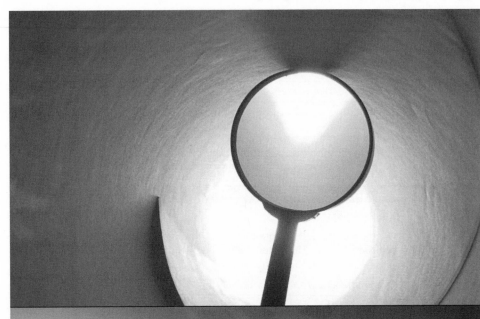

1. Publication Title	2. Publication Number								3. Filing Date
New Directions for Higher Education	0	2	7	1	–	0	5	6	0	10/1/2008

4. Issue Frequency	5. Number of Issues Published Annually	6. Annual Subscription Price
Quarterly	4	$209

7. Complete Mailing Address of Known Office of Publication *(Not printer) (Street, city, county, state, and ZIP+4®)*	Contact Person
Wiley Subscriptions Services, Inc. at Jossey-Bass, 989 Market St., San Francisco, CA 94103	Joe Schuman
	Telephone *(Include area code)* 415-782-3232

8. Complete Mailing Address of Headquarters or General Business Office of Publisher *(Not printer)*

Wiley Subscriptions Services, Inc., 111 River Street, Hoboken, NJ 07030

9. Full Names and Complete Mailing Addresses of Publisher, Editor, and Managing Editor *(Do not leave blank)*

Publisher *(Name and complete mailing address)*

Wiley Subscriptions Services, Inc., A Wiley Company at San Francisco, 989 Market St., San Francisco, CA 94103-1741

Editor *(Name and complete mailing address)*

Martin Kramer, 2807 Shasta Road, Berkeley, CA 94708

Managing Editor *(Name and complete mailing address)*

None

10. Owner *(Do not leave blank. If the publication is owned by a corporation, give the name and address of the corporation immediately followed by the names and addresses of all stockholders owning or holding 1 percent or more of the total amount of stock. If not owned by a corporation, give the names and addresses of the individual owners. If owned by a partnership or other unincorporated firm, give its name and address as well as those of each individual owner. If the publication is published by a nonprofit organization, give its name and address.)*

Full Name	Complete Mailing Address
Wiley Subscriptions Services	111 River Street, Hoboken, NJ
(see attached list)	

11. Known Bondholders, Mortgagees, and Other Security Holders Owning or Holding 1 Percent or More of Total Amount of Bonds, Mortgages, or Other Securities. If none, check box ➔ ☑ None

Full Name	Complete Mailing Address

12. Tax Status *(For completion by nonprofit organizations authorized to mail at nonprofit rates) (Check one)*
The purpose, function, and nonprofit status of this organization and the exempt status for federal income tax purposes:
☐ Has Not Changed During Preceding 12 Months
☐ Has Changed During Preceding 12 Months *(Publisher must submit explanation of change with this statement)*

PS Form **3526**, September 2006 *(Page 1 of 3 (Instructions Page 3))* PSN 7530-01-000-9931 PRIVACY NOTICE: See our privacy policy on www.usps.com

13. Publication Title	14. Issue Date for Circulation Data
New Directions for Higher Education	Summer 2008

15. Extent and Nature of Circulation			Average No. Copies Each Issue During Preceding 12 Months	No. Copies of Single Issue Published Nearest to Filing Date
a. Total Number of Copies *(Net press run)*			1115	1069
b. Paid Circulation *(By Mail and Outside the Mail)*	(1)	Mailed Outside-County Paid Subscriptions Stated on PS Form 3541(Include paid distribution above nominal rate, advertiser's proof copies, and exchange copies)	558	527
	(2)	Mailed In-County Paid Subscriptions Stated on PS Form 3541 (Include paid distribution above nominal rate, advertiser's proof copies, and exchange copies)	0	0
	(3)	Paid Distribution Outside the Mails Including Sales Through Dealers and Carriers, Street Vendors, Counter Sales, and Other Paid Distribution Outside USPS®	0	0
	(4)	Paid Distribution by Other Classes of Mail Through the USPS (e.g. First-Class Mail®)	0	0
c. Total Paid Distribution *(Sum of 15b (1), (2),(3), and (4))*			558	527
d. Free or Nominal Rate Distribution *(By Mail and Outside the Mail)*	(1)	Free or Nominal Rate Outside-County Copies lincluded on PS Form 3541	42	33
	(2)	Free or Nominal Rate In-County Copies Included on PS Form 3541	0	0
	(3)	Free or Nominal Rate Copies Mailed at Other Classes Through the USPS (e.g. First-Class Mail)	0	0
	(4)	Free or Nominal Rate Distribution Outside the Mail (Carriers or other means)	0	0
e. Total Free or Nominal Rate Distribution *(Sum of 15d (1), (2), (3) and (4))*			42	33
f. Total Distribution *(Sum of 15c and 15e)*		▶	600	560
g. Copies not Distributed *(See Instructions to Publishers #4 (page #3))*		▶	515	509
h. Total *(Sum of 15f and g)*		▶	1115	1069
i. Percent Paid *(15c divided by 15f times 100)*		▶	93%	94%

16. Publication of Statement of Ownership
☐ If the publication is a general publication, publication of this statement is required. Will be printed in the _Winter 2008_ issue of this publication. ☐ Publication not required.

17. Signature and Title of Editor, Publisher, Business Manager, or Owner	Date
Susan E. Lewis, VP & Publisher - Periodicals *(signature)*	10/1/2008

I certify that all information furnished on this form is true and complete. I understand that anyone who furnishes false or misleading information on this form or who omits material or information requested on the form may be subject to criminal sanctions (including fines and imprisonment) and/or civil sanctions (including civil penalties).

PS Form **3526**, September 2006 *(Page 2 of 3)*